The Song in the Night

According to the Melody in the Accents of the Hebrew Text

by

Bob MacDonald

Energion Publications

Gonzalez, Florida, U.S.A.

2016

The Song in the Night

All Scripture translations are the author's.

This work was done between 2013 and 2016 with the help of the GX/LEAF software from Anthony Macauley Associates with particular thanks to Vishnu Singh and David Driver.

This book has been aided by research during a Community Fellowship in the first quarter of 2016 at the Centre for Studies in Religion and Society, University of Victoria.

ISBN10: 1-63199-292-9
ISBN13: 978-1-63199-292-6

Library of Congress Control Number: 2016959349

Energion Publications
P. O. Box 841
Gonzalez, Florida, 32560

850-525-3916
www.energionpubs.com

10 9 8 7 6 5 4 3 2 1 0

10 November 2016 15:38

What they are saying about The Song in the Night.

This is a very interesting, user-friendly publication! I initially opened it in my IPhone but found myself reading it with great interest, not least because Bob explains difficult issues so clearly.

Susan Gillingham, Fellow and Tutor in Theology, Professor of the Hebrew Bible, Worcester College Oxford

Bob MacDonald brings to the song of the Scriptures a meticulous attention to detail, an eye for imagery and symbol, and a heart for the feel and tone of the text that inspires the reader to look with fresh eyes at these ancient sacred writings. He enlivens the story with beauty and faith that is evident on every page.

Christopher Page, Rector, St Philip's Oak Bay

For several years now Bob has on occasion treated our congregation to a taste of how Jesus himself may have heard the Scriptures sung in the Synagogue. Congregations integrating the music of the Hebrew Scriptures into their worship in this way will be deeply enriched, not just because it brings us closer to the historical setting of Jesus' experience, not just by the beauty of the music, but most importantly by how these settings invite us to hear the word of God anew. We are indebted to Bob's work to make this possible.

Rev. Dr. Travis O'Brian, Rector, St Barnabas Anglican Church; Director of Anglican Studies, Vancouver School of Theology

Bob MacDonald's book is clearly both a work of detailed scholarship and a labor of love. With the help of computer technology, MacDonald, building on the work of Haik-Vantoura and an important key provided by Psalm 114, turns the puzzling markings that pervade manuscripts in the Hebrew Bible into music. I have no doubt that the years to come will witness not only vigorous debate about this procedure among scholars, but also performances and adaptations of the music MacDonald provides. Even if someone is skeptical about the interpretation of these symbols as musical notation, or this specific interpretation of them, they can still benefit from something MacDonald does that is, to my knowledge, unprecedented. By recognizing that these are performance markings, we can tell that certain passages in the Hebrew Bible were performed in the same way, using comparable melodic lines. And so we have here very old evidence of how cantors viewed texts as related to one another, and depicted that relationship through the very act of melodic recitation. The importance of this work for those interested in the interpretation and reception history of the Bible, as well as the more specific field of the Bible and music, should not be underestimated.

Dr. James F. McGrath, Clarence L. Goodwin Chair in New Testament Language and Literature Department of Philosophy & Religion, Butler University

The Cover

The image on the cover is the west face of Old Jerusalem by night with the Tower of David on the left, taken in 2010 by the author.

The music is obscured on the cover like the hand signals in the ancient manuscripts. In the book, the music is clear so that all this ancient prose and poetry might be sung as well as muttered.

For Oliver and Benjamin

Anyone who reads from the Bible without a melody
or recites the Mishnah without a tune, to him applies the verse

Ezekiel 20.25

ve - gam   a - ni   na - ta - ti   la - hem   chu - qim   lo   to -
And moreover I my - self   have   giv - en / them / statutes that are   not

vim   u - mish - pa - tim   lo   yich - yu ba - hem
good,   and   judg - ments that will   not   live / in   them.

R. Yohanen in b. Megilla 32a.

Preface

This volume outlines a special beauty of the text of the Hebrew Bible. The music in these pages is derived entirely and consistently from the text of the Hebrew. The compact hand signals embedded syllable by syllable in the text of the Hebrew were transcribed automatically by computer program and the resulting musical scores have not been altered except to add a translated libretto.

The decoding of these signals follows the deciphering key inferred by Suzanne Haïk-Vantoura. Her inductive approach to the musical information structure of the accents from the 20th century has given us a new way of appreciating the ancient Scriptures, both poetry and prose.

One aspect of this new way is that we can now imagine what it might have been like for the ancients to hear and perform their Scripture as an art song. It is as if we *seekers*, light years away from earth, have reached out, snared, and decoded the equi-tempered frequencies of the golden (*snitch*) record that led Explorer II into the universe. And, as with Bach, it will take us time to appreciate the depth of the expression of the music.

In my first book on the Bible, I followed the thesis that the book of Psalms is not a random collection of songs but a carefully constructed story. In this second book, it can be seen that the Bible is not only a set of stories to be read but also a carefully constructed and beautiful song to be heard.

With over 6,000 pages of music to choose from, I have collated an excerpt from the ancient story with a few examples, a few of thousands of choices. It is a story that you can read and sing. It is a story that will show you a new way of hearing these ancient texts. It is a song for us in the night.

All 6,000+ pages of the automated drafts of the music are available online at http://meafar.blogspot.ca/p/music.html. I am coming to the conclusion that no serious analysis of the content of the Hebrew Bible can neglect its music and the place of that music in the chapter and in other parts of Scripture.

Bob MacDonald

Victoria, B.C. Lent 2016

Contents

List of Illustrations

Rejoice in God O ye Tongues: Give the glory to the Lord and the Lamb
Nations and languages And every Creature In which is the breath of Life
Let man and beast appear before him, and magnify his name together

from the opening of Rejoice in the Lamb, Benjamin Britten

Jubilate Agno, Fragment A, by Christopher Smart

Foreword

You have in your hands a readable music book. Reading a book with music between the paragraphs is a little different from reading a scholarly tome or a novel. It is not an exercise in speed. The eye allows us to see quickly, but the ear demands presence and time to hear the musical phrases in their sequence. The sweetness of the music makes this book a little like a layered cookie.

Chapters 1 and 7 and the Appendices are somewhat technical. You need to read them and come back to them but you don't need to read them first. They are the crunchy part of the cookie. They describe the struggle to interpret the signs. Chapters 2 through 6 scan the canonical history in five stages: Creation, Escape, Home, Exile, Restoration. They are the sweet inner part of the cookie, that many I know would rather eat first. They summarize the story of the God of Israel and the people of Israel with many musical examples. Their music is an integral part of the narrative of the book. All the examples are in line and meant to be read and the performance imagined by non-musician or musician in the normal sequential act of reading a book.

Chapter 1, Languages, introduces the problem, a puzzle with over 300,000 pieces set for us by our ancestors. The puzzle is still in the box. We have only in the past 40 years begun to see how to unpack it. Many people have tried in the last 1000 years, but their attempts have been piecemeal and have not been widely known. So chapter 1 gives us a language for describing the pieces. We can see how each piece is shaped and we learn how to fit them together given their shapes. The primary language is musical. There is also some technical language and some polemical language as we encounter both the perceived difficulty of the puzzle and some resistance to a musical solution.

Chapter 2 is Creation. Creation is approached through the opening act of Genesis 1 combined with the character of Leviathan in the epic poem of the book of Job. It is the music that invites the comparison.

Chapter 3 is Escape. Escape from the house of servitude is approached from the call of Moses to the building of the sanctuary. Atonement and Oneness are introduced and the desire of Yahweh to find a home and of those who have escaped to make such a home for their God. The chapter ends with the commandment.

Chapter 4 is Home. Home begins with the integrity of Samuel and continues to the character and memory of the monarchy and the building of the temple. The chapter ends with riddle and parable.

Chapter 5 is Exile. Exile begins with the protest language of the prophets and the honesty of lament. It ends with the character of the acts of a servant.

Chapter 6 is Restoration. Restoration begins with trust and return and continues with consolation and redemption. The five middle chapters conclude with praise.

Chapter 7 is an introduction to the deciphering key that allows this elegant musical solution to the puzzle. It contains some suggestions on performance practice.

Within the middle chapters are many single verses of music and a few larger sections that can be performed. Appendix 1 contains four full sections of the lectionary that have been performed in the context of a service. Appendix 2 compares other suggested solutions to the puzzle. Appendix 3 shows how statistics confirm the capacity and clarity of the suggested solution.

1. Languages

I have come to this writing as a musician, as a programmer, and as a student of Hebrew. I also arrive here as one who is interested in what Christians call the Old Testament and Jews the Tanach. This is a set of books that most of us find somewhat impenetrable. What does it have to teach us and how will we learn from it?

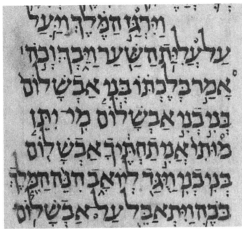
Figure 1 The Aleppo codex, 2 Samuel 19.1

First, look at Figure 1. The scribe loved the giraffe-necked ells (ל). "The Aleppo Codex is a full manuscript of the entire Bible, which was written in about 930. For more than a thousand years, the manuscript was preserved in its entirety in important Jewish communities in the Near East: Tiberias, Jerusalem, Egypt, and in the city of Aleppo in Syria. However, in 1947, after the United Nations Resolution establishing the State of Israel, it was damaged in riots that broke out in Syria."[1]

In Figure 2 you can focus on the third and fourth lines of Figure 1 with a few words of the same text typed. (בני אבשלום, beni Abshalom, my son Absalom). The relationship of the signs to the letters is easier to see in typewritten form because it separates the lines more clearly. Note all three parts of the text: the consonants, the vowels, and the cantillation signs or accents (circled). See Chapter 7 for the full alphabet.

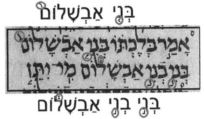
Figure 2 Highlighting the accents

Note that some of the cantillation signs are *above* the letters and some are *below*. This was the first of the clues that was pointed out and followed by the French organist and composer, Suzanne Haïk-Vantoura. The second clue she followed is that the signs below the letters occur in *every* verse, but the signs above *are entirely absent* in about 14% of the verses of the Bible. She deduced that the signs below the letters were more important and she inferred from their placement and frequency of use that they constituted a musical scale. She considered that she had reconstructed what she hoped is the original music of the Temple in Jerusalem.[2] I am not certain that she is completely right in her claim, but what she has done is to give us a key that unlocks the windows of our ears as we listen afresh to the words of the Hebrew Bible. Applying her key to the image of the five words in Figure 2 gives the result in Figure 3. I have summarized her work in Chapter 7.

---

[1] http://www.aleppocodex.org/links/6.html

[2] Ce sont les chants des LEVITES, ceux perpétués au Temple de JERUSALEM sous l'impulsion de DAVID et selon sa gestuelle (from the frontispiece of the French edition).

Figure 3 A portion of 2 Samuel 19.1

Coded language

In 2010, the theory I have illustrated in these pages was first presented to me by David Mitchell at the Oxford conference on the Psalms in 2010 convened by Susan Gillingham. The signs are so regular, it is feasible to write a program in a computer language to read the text and apply a set of rules to produce a musical score. Note that I am not considering reading the text with a computer program to infer a set of rules. That is not impossible. But having inferred a set of rules, deriving the music is relatively simple. But which set of rules? This requires testing them against the data of the text itself.

I was intrigued to find a musical score encoded deliberately in the text of an ancient collection of documents. When I began my study of the text, the marks that were neither consonant nor vowel were incomprehensible to me. The names of the approximately two dozen marks were so foreign and their usage rules as stated in various treatises were so complex that I could not understand what was asserted about them and their precedence over each other.

I supposed that others understood the hierarchy of accents that aided grammatical parsing, but it seemed to me that the rules of the hierarchy were constantly being broken, and the more I read about these marks, the less I believed that anyone, even the writers, understood what they were claiming about them. When, on the other hand, the signs are decoded according to the instructions implicit in their placement, they are no longer contradictory, and, through the derived music, they shape the words outside the bounds of grammar and punctuation[3] alone.

The design principle of Occam's razor, that one should prefer the explanation with the fewest assumptions, has two corollaries: 1. It is futile to do with many things what a few would accomplish more simply. 2. An interpretation that uses more of the information that is implied in the tool set is to be preferred to one that uses less. Haïk-Vantoura's thesis clearly uses more information implicit in the signs than traditional cantillation. A good theory should also predict new results that would not otherwise have been seen.

Musical language

The names of the accents in Hebrew are unfamiliar to English speakers and even to many Hebrew speakers. The accents in traditional cantillation have limited tonal association. Traditional cantillation associates a melisma with one sign or a consecutive pair of signs. The tonality of the chant is generally the same for all accents in a particular space, for Torah, a major tonality, for Haftarah, a minor tonality.

---

[3] The emphasis in the literature on *punctuation* makes us fail to see that the role of the accents is first related to *syllable-stress*, and secondarily to *word separation*. The music carries this phrasing into sentences, verses, and groups of verses.

In contrast with this, once the score is revealed as having multiple reciting notes by using more of the information implicit in the placement of the signs, we can see and hear the signs in quite a different way and describe them more fully with the language of music (Figure 4): tonic, supertonic (the note above the tonic), mode, even major or minor, mediant, a third above the tonic, subdominant (the fourth note above the tonic), dominant (the fifth note above the tonic), submediant, the sixth above the tonic, sixths, sevenths, augmented and diminished, octaves, triads and so on.

Figure 4 Musical terms for the notes of a scale

The tonic is the note that when you return to it, you feel like you are home. It is the starting note for a verse, unless the first syllable of the verse specifies another. The subdominant plays a major role in most verses (93% of them to be exact). It is a point of rest. The supertonic is used as an additional rest point in the Psalms, Proverbs, and the speeches of Job (in about 10% of their verses). These names all have tonal memory behind their definitions.

Haïk-Vantoura's key allows us to reconstruct a musical performance of the text. It may suggest a tone of voice that is quite different from what we hear when reading without music. It draws us away from the tonic in each verse and returns us at the end of each verse. It is not necessarily the major scale of Figure 4, but more likely one of many possible modal scales. Different modes will suit differing parts of the Scripture.

Extended markup language

The scores in this book and on the web site are created from the text of the Hebrew Bible via a web service to Tanach.us. In principle, no information is lost in the process. The text is transformed into Music XML by automation. XML is extended markup language. Music XML allows a musical score to be described in words.

For example, <note><pitch><step>A</step><octave>4</octave>... You can see that this is very similar to the HTML language used to build web pages.

Most music programs support reading such a description and interpreting it into a regular musical score. I use Musescore 2.0.2 through which I have manually added the translated lyrics. There is nothing magical about any part of such programming. And it would equally not have been magical for the musicians of 2000 years ago, who as with some teachers today, regularly used the sign language of hand signals (called cheironomy from the Greek for hand, χέρι) to indicate the pitch of the notes of a melody.

Hebrew language

The Hebrew language is written right to left and in square script. To accommodate this in a book that is written left to right, and scores that are left to right, the Hebrew text is above the musical line word by word. Each word is read right to left, but the words themselves are left to right so that they are placed over the music that they determine.

An automated transcription of the Hebrew is written into the first line of lyrics, followed by a second line of translated lyrics in a close and concordant translation that can be assigned to the shape of the musical line.[4] Psalm 6 is inscribed *For the leader, on strings, over octaves.* The inscription is an integral part of the music. We can sing the stage directions as well as the play itself.

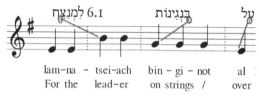

Figure 5 Interpreting the accents - 1

The score embedded in the hand signals in the text contains all the information that the program uses to construct the music. In this snippet of the music we have a leap of a fifth from the tonic to the dominant, then a descending minor triad. So the first two words determine three notes through the specific accents, given a default starting note of E.

The Hebrew is parsed by the program syllable by syllable. The notes and ornaments in their sequences are clearly associated with each syllable. The last few words show an ornament and the changes in reciting note that return us to the tonic.

Figure 6 Interpreting the accents - 2

Polemical language

There are many articles online with the Hebrew names of the accents and the descriptions of their workings. These do not see or use all the information available in the signs and their placement. Many will have learned from the classic and very clearly written 19th century work by William Wickes: *A treatise on the accentuation of the three so-called poetical books on the Old Testament, Psalms, Proverbs, and Job, with an appendix containing the treatise, assigned to R. Jehuda Ben-Bil'am, on the same subject, in the original Arabic.* Wickes wrote two treatises, one on the three books and one on the 21 books.

Wickes was a counterfoil for me in my learning from the 21st century thousand-page volume on cantillation by Joshua R. Jacobson, *Chanting the Hebrew Bible, The Complete Guide to the Art of Cantillation.* Jacobson spells out the melismas for each sign and pairs of signs in modern traditional Jewish cantillation in North America. This is consistent in itself and different from the rules I have applied. Traditional cantillation has little if any concept of a change in reciting note and as a result of this

---

[4] There is no 'right' underlay of a translation of the Hebrew. In all cases one must make decisions as to which syllables to place on which notes.

limitation, *one will fail to hear connections between verses.* (See Appendix 2 for a worked example using both Jacobson and Haïk-Vantoura.)

William Wickes studied many manuscripts directly. He begins his first thesis: "I soon saw that even our best texts need correction, as far as the accents are concerned; and that, without a correct text, I could not hope to establish any rules on a satisfactory basis. I therefore visited the leading Libraries of Europe, and collated, as far as seemed necessary, most of the known MSS" (1871 :preface).

We see from this that he is searching for the rules that govern the placement of accents. Here he is doing what each of us might do in order to understand the coding. He differs in access to many libraries from Haïk-Vantoura, who worked by musical inference. He differs in technology from the 21st century investigator in that he cannot have access by database to all the data from one source. There may well be errors in my source, but the volume of data will largely render them harmless to analysis.

Wickes makes several regulatory claims. One that would be understood in traditional cantillation is this: "Logically, a verse may be closely connected with the one preceding or following it; but musically and accentually no such connection exists." (1881 :23). He is oriented towards his dichotomy model whereby every phrase decomposes itself into two using the disjunctive accents (1887 :20). As such he is stopping in the middle of a musical phrase rather than hearing its completion. Also he is biased toward the dissociation of each verse from any other "Each section or verse was then treated as an independent whole; and, whatever its connection in sense with the verse preceding or the verse following, had its musical division assigned to it, quite irrespectively of them." (1887 :27). This is not a necessary assumption. And assumption is what it is.

Dresher (1994 :6) is on the right track when he writes of the accents as a Prosodic system. Prosody is defined as singing to speech. And it is the phrasing that is critical. What unsung prosody can miss, however, is the tone of voice. This too is critical to the interpretive approach. Dresher makes the same claim as Wickes, however, when he writes "No prosodic or phonological phenomena span more than one verse" (1994 :16). This is simply too limiting for music and is demonstrably untrue.

These claims are testable. Perhaps one exception would prove that such a general rule cannot stand. But there is not just one, there are examples on every page of Scripture that deny such a restriction of the role of the accents. The music of this deciphering key sings relationships within verses and between verses and chapters. Just note, to begin with, those verses that do not begin on the tonic. This is a listening skill that is quickly learned and easier than describing a sequence of accents. Then note the ornaments and their usage. Haïk-Vantoura's music is a significant advance over considering that the accents are confined to grammatical relationships within one verse.

Helmut Richter[5] has explanations of the non-musical interpretation of the accents. Such tradition occasionally results in a clear statement of grammatical purpose of the cantillation marks, but only clear within its own limited assumptions. Then he writes what must be interpreted as a complete escape clause: "the real nesting levels stay nowhere constant and can jump up and down by arbitrary amounts."

---

[5] http://www.mechon-mamre.org/c/hr/intro.htm

An article by Emmanuel Rubin from the University of Massachusetts, summarizes the work on the accents in the latter half of the 20th century as "almost all didactic". He writes that "contemporary informants only tell us what we already know" (1993 :1). But he does not mention Haïk-Vantoura. In fact he cites authorities and tradition that would seem to preclude any thought of beauty in the recitation of the text: "To the extent that our melodic 'traditions' are song-like, they are not those of the Masoretes, but of the last few centuries of Western art music. Cantillation was not intended to be 'natural'; rather, it is explicitly artificial and ritualistic" (1993 :10). I take this as negative, but artifice and ritual are both aspects of beauty. The attribution of negative intent to these signs will continue to deny the possibility of music or song to the ancient world. It is neither a necessary reading, nor a necessary assumption. The authorities that he cites all labour under the impression that the Masoretes sought to impose and reinforce *meaning* with pauses and stresses in selected places in the text. This is a very strange objective for a community that is characterized by weighing and sifting words and letters to achieve a multi-faceted interaction with a variety of inferences from the same text (i.e. a community that does *not* wish to impose a singular meaning onto the text).

Adler and Cohen in their brief article in the Jewish Encyclopedia put down 18th and 19th century reconstruction attempts in one sentence: "these investigators did not combine that acquaintance at once with Hebrew grammar and history and with synagogue music". The first 2 parts of this critique do not apply to Haïk-Vantoura's reconstruction, and the third is spurious if the synagogue tradition has so diverged as to be a distraction on the way to a goal that it could dimly support only when the goal is achieved.

The Hebrew Student begins an issue like this: "The supposed authority of the accents is very dependent on their supposed antiquity. The accents form now a part of all our printed Bibles. The fact is curious. Why are they there, and by what authority? Here on the one hand we are in danger of falling under the influence of a derationalizing superstition, and on the other, under a supercilious flippancy, the well-beloved child of ignorance" (1883 :164-169). This opening of the article is not promising, but the writer ends the first long paragraph of prejudice and innuendo with this more promising note: "As all Jewish intentions looked in one direction, that of preserving inviolate their divinely inspired Scriptures, it is probable that if we can really read the intention of the accents, we shall not have lost, but gained in our esteem for human reverence and religious care, as well as in our understanding of the Bible."

The classic definition of the accents is noted in this anonymous piece: "The manner of applying these rhetorical points, called accents, is tactical, and resembles the marshalling of an army; and therefore they are ranged by grammarians under five classes, of different qualities, one of superiors, and four of inferiors; and for distinction sake, they call them emperors, kings, major lords, minor lords, and ministers, or servants: The emperors (two in number) and two of the kings, one in prose, the other in verse, are absolute lords; all the rest are subordinate, some to one absolute lord, and some to another, and some are common, and serve any lord" (1744 :29).

The author is determined to prove using both Hebrew and the Septuagint that the accents and vowel points were written on the tables of the Law at Sinai (the broken tables being Exodus, and the second tables, Deuteronomy). It would be another book to explore this clearly devotional even if misguided treatise. Besides, the black fire on white fire may be an army, but it is also a song.

In Gesenius' Hebrew Grammar, he writes in a footnote, "The division of the disjunctive accents in Imperatores, Reges, Duces, Comites, which became common amongst Christian grammarians, originated in the Scrutinium S. S. ex accentibus of Sam. Bohlius, Rostock 1636, and, as the source of manifold confusion, had better be given up" (1910 :59n). He is in turn criticized for his limited remarks on the accents by Margolis (1911 :29).

The article, *The Masoretes and the Punctuation of Biblical Hebrew*, Levy and Robinson (2002), is typical of the complex entrenched explanations for the system of *accents* as *punctuation*. If a data designer came to me with such a proposal, I would ask for a simplification and reduction of the number of signs. The design as described has more symbols and sequences of symbols than would be required for the conjunctions and disjunctions in a system of punctuation.[6] But it is not too complex for a musical interpretation. And it shows itself capable of sufficient variety of application to the possibilities of musical expression. I have noted also a tendency in reading strategies both with traditional cantillation and with grammatical models, that require the reader to look ahead. Hierarchic analysis is one such strategy. Haïk-Vantoura's deciphering key does not require a look-ahead processor. The information for singing is contained in the accent itself. As with letters and words, it is good to look ahead, but it is not mandatory.

There is division in response to Haïk-Vantoura's work. She was commended by her musical teachers and peers, Messaien, Duruflé, and Dupré, but Werner (1982 :924) considers her book "the perfect mixture of ignorance and confusion." Her thesis that the signs below the letters are functionally different from those above seems inevitable now that it has been noted. The following step of accepting the idea of a change in reciting note is not far behind. DeHoop (2013 :12) mentions this in an almost offhand comment concerning Oriental music: "the point is where the pitch of the voice is to be raised or lowered in order that each sentence should be understood correctly", but he does not suggest a change in reciting note.

Conclusion

Tradition knows that the signs are somehow both exegetical and musical. Tradition also recognizes that the musical meaning has been lost (Wickes 1881 :2n). It then assumes that grammatical analysis or punctuation is the dominant use for the accents (ibid. :3n). If I have to read a complex treatise with 25 or 30 unpronounceable words and contorted simplification about the conjunctive and disjunctive hierarchical roles of diacritics, then I simply won't do it. If I have to listen to transparent, dramatic, and beautiful music and don't have to be told what I am hearing because it catches my ear and spirit, then I will hear and love the result. What you will hear in this book is transparent without all the explanations of how it is done. The rules are easily learned. Sight singing is easily learned. Lessons sung with these instructions are dramatic. The result is beauty and clarity. I hope through the music to focus on greater engagement with the sensibility of the text and its expressiveness.

---

[6] It is fair to say that I am slightly overstating the case. The signs could be syntactical (punctuation) if we include parentheses and invent some other signs to bring the required total to 19 or so.

The Song in the Night

I would note also that no accent is hierarchic under any condition. All notes in a musical phrase serve each other and the phrase is not a phrase without all of them. The idea of continuous dichotomy should be removed from discussion. Music is subject to more nuanced shape than a hierarchy, a concept that is overused in most professions.

You cannot make marmalade without soaking the seeds, cutting up the oranges, and complementing their bitterness with sweetness. Time then to cut through contorted explanation and soak in the energy of the pectin deep within the seeds and add the sweetness of the song in the night to the bitter pulp and skin.

My title track, *the song in the night*, is from Psalm 42.

PSALM 42

These psalms, 42[7] and 43, are a single poem in two parts, and a corporate lament expressed in the first person singular (I, my). They are followed by a lament expressed in the first person plural (we, us).

PSALM 44

These three psalms together give us insight into the reality of exile. (See further below under Lament.) It is night.

The five chapters that follow, Creation, Escape, Home, Exile, Restoration are an introductory journey through the story in the Bible via musical examples. Each example, either through a keyword or a musical shape, suggested a related verse of the story and so determined a rough path through the downs and ups of 6000+ pages of music from the Hebrew Bible telling the story of a people chosen to be the

---

[7] All chapter numbers and verse numbers are traditional Hebrew numbering. Chapter and verse numbers will sometimes differ from English bibles.

canonical example. If this is too simple an approach to the ancient tales, let me add that the story is also meant for us to learn from, that through it we might have hope in the face of our difficult global situation. The ancients did not see our 'world' but they learned and recorded their failures with great diligence and now we can also hear rather than just see and explain their world. Perhaps we might also learn from it.

There are very many possible paths through the story and I would welcome more exploration of the data. I have not yet examined all the text and music. I am able using the database to give some statistics on the usage of shapes of the musical line. I have not yet asked all the questions one might ask of a database or of the choices that the 'composer(s)' of the accents might have considered.

Throughout the story, I will examine the music, including analysis of the reciting notes and how they might be heard as tone of voice. I will look at specific ornamentation and how it emphasizes or points out certain characteristics of the text, as if the composer was telling us to note something, perhaps in the grammar, perhaps in the word, or in a structural feature.

The words are also written for us to learn something we may not be able to measure. So I have found invitation, correction, rebuke, redemption, delight, pleasure, and hope, to name just a few things that go beyond what I can describe. It seems to me that wherever I place a passage, its applicability goes beyond that particular place in the story. It is as if all parts of the story are contemporaneous, both then and now. Would I treat other stories this way?

2. Creation

Beginnings

When I first heard this music, it sounded familiar, as if I had heard it before, yet it was new. But for all its foreignness, a two-year old child can hear it. Try singing to such a child this next example, the opening verse of the Torah. The pause for rest on the subdominant and the start and end on the tonic will not require much explanation.

So let us begin at the beginning, or at least some where or when in the middle of beginning. The first verse of the Bible is a major triad with a mid-verse cadence on the subdominant. The mid-verse cadence in the Hebrew is on the last syllable of God. Then the music returns to the tonic via the supertonic and the major third.

GENESIS 1

Pitch the music where it is comfortable for you. The opening major triad is, in the traditional solfege, doh, mi, sol, followed by the subdominant, fa (e-g#-B-A). Pause.

Then descend a major third to re (f), then (in this mode) go up the characteristic augmented second from re to mi (g#). Then back to re and back to doh.

Always take your time at the cadence. Count to two to give yourself and your hearer time to think about why the rest is on that particular word in that particular sentence.

In the beginning of God's creating what? Take up the tune again: *the heavens and the earth*. This second half of the phrase is the direct object of the first half of the phrase. We know that it is the direct object from the word 'eit'. This two-letter word is spelt alef-taf. It is comprised of the first (א) and last (ת) letters of the Hebrew alphabet. It signifies that the direct object of the verb follows. There are two direct objects in the phrase, *hashamayim*, the heavens, and *ha'arets*, the earth. To match the rhythm of the Hebrew, we might translate the phrase as; of *both the heavens and also the earth*. But generally speaking, the direct object marker את is not translated.

Why didn't I translate as usual: *in the beginning, God created*? There are a lot of good reasons. In Hebrew, it is often the case that a word ending in 't' indicates a special form of the noun that says 'more to come'. In this case, the single word bereshit, is 'in the beginning of', not just 'in the beginning'. There is a suggestion in this form of the verb 'to begin' that creation continues and that time is different from the time-line that we might imagine, as if God 'created' and then just let the clockwork happen.

Music too is more than a single note. Music gathers words into a single phrase that holds the beginning in the end and makes time, in a sense, stand still. There is much more that could be said about the heavens and our earth, our land, even our own individual piece of the ground which we know as body, a body with ears that can hear the music it sings, a body with heart that can know the singer of the music, a body with eyes that can process the information in the music, the text, and its history.

So *the beginning* is more than a distant big bang, and more than a distant act of speech. It can be heard as a continuing presence and therefore a promising end, even as we would expect from a musical composition.

This opening snippet of music gathers 18 syllables into two phrases. The first word shows a change in reciting note on the third syllable. So we move from e to g#, from doh to mi. The second syllable of the second word shows a sign that moves us to a sol (B). Then the first of this pair of phrases has a rest point in the middle (fa, A) marked by the atnah (^) under the third syllable of Elohim.

We rest on *God's* creating. Even in the middle of a thought, we rest.

The fourth word, the single syllable direct object marker, shows that we move to f (re). Then the third syllable of *hashamayim*, the heavens, moves us back to g# (mi). The second syllable of the sixth word, the second direct object marker, moves us back to f (re), and then we reach the tonic e (doh), again on the silluq on the middle syllable of the seventh word.

So we have a musical movement from tonic to subdominant in the first phrase. Each stressed syllable follows the dashed bar line which always occurs at a change in reciting note. Then a musical movement from the rest point back to the tonic. Each phrase has three stresses and each leads to the end of the phrase as one would expect of music.

Here is another example from the first verse of Job.

Note how similar the shape of the music is to the first verse of Genesis. Yet there is a certain lilt to the opening of Job as if it was announcing a story. And a story that is meant to recall the opening of Genesis. There is a 'once upon a time' with it. The approach to the cadence is the same as Genesis but it is preceded by two notes that are not the tonic or 'home' note.[8] Then there is a comment on high and low notes identifying the self-same Job as complete, (*tam*) and upright (*yashar*). Then to close and come to the musical 'home', the music is similar to the second half of Genesis verse 1.[9]

---

[8] The Book of Job as coded in the Leningrad codex does not start on the tonic (the E of the scale). Psalms, Proverbs, and Deuteronomy are the only other books that start on a note other than the tonic.

[9] You might think these are common approaches to the mid verse cadence and return paths to the home note. In some sense they are common, as common as the implied harmonic structure. But the notes of the whole phrase are not so common. Genesis

Music has a significant impact on memory. One gets used to the various motifs. The octave scale stays in the memory of the singer. To help distinguish these two verses, note that Genesis 1.1 has no recitation on the rest note, but immediately drops a major third to the second. In contrast Job 1.1 after the rest continues for two syllables on the rest to begin its elaboration of the character of its protagonist, Job.

Here is a bit of encouragement from Psalm 33 with the same opening theme in a major mode. This old song is new. Psalm 33 is unique in Book 1 of the Psalter. It is the only psalm between 3 and 41 to have no inscription.[10] And it is among those special psalms that are followed by an acrostic, an alphabetic poem. It is the first time *a new song* is mentioned in the Psalms.

PSALM 33

shi-ru lo shir cha – dash hei – ti-vu na – gein bit-ru – ah
Sing to him a new / song, well – practiced perform with jub-il – ation.

Leviathan

The scope of Job as a book responding to creation in Genesis is clear from Job's first speech. Job slights his day: Perish! day in which I was born ... *let it be darkness.* Perhaps it is not an accident that the opening verses were similar.

JOB 3

ha – yom ha-hu ye – hi cho-shek al yid-re – shei-hu e – lo-ah mi-
That day let it be dark – ness / let God not search for it / from a –

ma – al ve – al to – fa a – lav ne – ha – rah
bove / nor let a sun – beam / on it shine.

This is the exact opposite of the first fiat from God with its mid-verse rest on *light.*

1.1 is one of 423 verses (out of 23,150) that have that exact form, e-g#-B-A. It is one of 906 verses that return from the subdominant to the tonic with its exact final four notes. Only 26 of these share the approach and the return. There are, as in all music, common patterns as well as uniqueness of phrase in the larger context. Job 1.1 is one of seven verses with this particular approach d-f- e-g#-B-A to the mid verse cadence. The others are Exodus 34.14, Numbers 2.32, Isaiah 5.18, Isaiah 29.15, Jonah 3.2, and Qohelet 7.12.

[10] All the other psalms from 3 to 41 are of David. You might exclude Psalm 10 which has no inscription, but inherits the inscription from Psalm 9, for it is the second half of that broken acrostic.

GENESIS 1

Surely a battle is brewed in this story. Light comes to each of us on our day of birth and there is trouble on every doorstep. And as for the night that precedes the day,

JOB 3

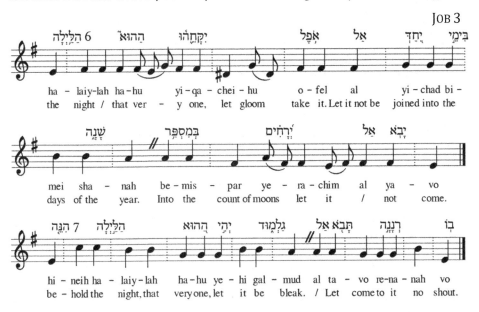

And now we hear Job's cry for reinforcements against that night that the child was conceived, a cry against his opening his eyes on trouble, a cry against the full scope of misery that is evident in the world, and though it is particularly his world in his story, he need not be relegated to a lone voice in a distant land or a distant time. This bodily cry from one can speak for all, as if all were in the one body in the one place.

Ultimately, though the speeches are full of many words, Job for his stubborn insistence is commended (perhaps in a somewhat understated manner) by Yahweh when Yahweh criticizes the three friends of Job for their inadequate statements about God.

JOB 42

The friends use third person explanation of the God they appeal to for their claims. They maintain their distance. So they have not spoken *what is prepared*, or alternatively, *what is established*. This segment of the music is high and angular. What is the storyteller signifying with the intervals? Job's speeches, in contrast to those of his friends, transform into prayer. We often see how he changes without warning from third person descriptive to second person direct address. He is one of very few characters in the Hebrew Bible outside the Psalms to use this characteristic of Hebrew prayer language.

JOB 14

Here there is a sense of the subdued Leviathan that is Job. Though Job is shattered by the fierceness of the violence against him, his response to it is both determined and honest. The form of verse 4 is chiastic with respect to the music e-B-g-B-e. The middle is important in a circular structure. And here it is the clean-unclean axis. In Yahweh's response to Job, *Leviathan* is a monster but with fluttering *eyelids*, and even his sneeze is key to the *light* of *dawn* that he wished had not been.

JOB 41

These words, the end of the conversation, are among many in the speeches of Yahweh that repeat the same words that Job used in chapter 3. They provide a frame for the whole post-traumatic conversation among the 6 speaking actors.

Leviathan finds his heads splintered for food for people of wild places. And this is celebrated by the poet as an act of Yahweh in creating the world.

PSALM 74

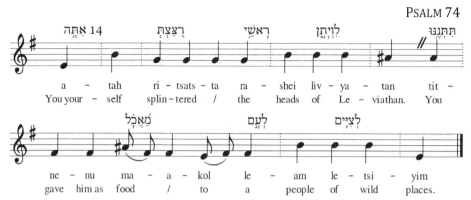

Psalm 74 is one of the collection of laments in Books 3 and 4 of the Psalter that reflect the exile of Judah and Israel.

While trouble occurs everywhere and at many times, the exile focuses the problem. The story of Job, like the story of Israel, is food to the people of the whole world.

Leviathan is God's companion in laughter.

PSALM 104

The music of Leviathan records the battle of the creator with chaos. But like Job, Leviathan's story has a happy ending. Part of the translator's battle with chaos is with the words. As I set them, the rhythm of the ornaments invites a different reading and a different word order or sentence structure. I must give in.

My parameters for translating are very restrictive. I want concordance so that repeated words in Hebrew are matched with repetitions in English, but I have some conceptual and cultural barriers. I will not knowingly reuse an English root for two differing Hebrew roots, but some Hebrew words demand a plurality of glosses. I want to allow myself the odd creative and free impulse, but the music demands a reasonable pattern match.

Also, one must be careful with close 'literal' translations of foreign tongues! Here from my Hebrew coach is a more radical reading of the verse referred to in the rabbinic comment on the dedicatory page: And what? And I gave them "bad laws" that they chose not to live by the statutes?

There is freedom of thought even in the ancient tongue. So by all means, I say to myself, Be bound, and be free, but be sensible also.

3. Escape

Rescue

And now, for a change of pace, we take up the story of Israel on their way into Egypt from Canaan. When Jacob and his family went to Egypt they were a few people.

EXODUS 1

And in the story, the *names* of the families follow. But when they became many, there were disputes with their Egyptian hosts and they ended up in slavery. The people were in trouble and they needed to be rescued.

EXODUS 3

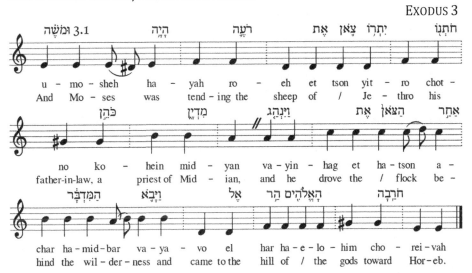

The rescue begins with Moses meeting a Mystery alone, behind the wilderness, near the hill of the gods over toward Horeb.

The gods? Well you might ask why I wrote 'the gods' rather than God. The word (אלוהים) might be with or without the definite article (ה), or the definite article might apply implicitly. Traditional translations pay little attention to the differences and sometimes I don't either. But often I do. In this particular case I don't think that capitalization applies either. There are no case distinctions in the letters in the Hebrew text. Sometimes I render 'the God' as 'the gods' or just as 'God' or even 'this God' though a different Hebrew would apply there (האלוהים הזה) but that sequence of letters never occurs in the text. Even when the two root words (god and this) occur in sequence, the 'this' always refers to what follows and not backward as if to qualify

The Song in the Night

God as one among many. It is likely that no qualification of God is required in such a form.

It is here, in a conversation in which Moses is addressed by name, that he is warned, and commissioned.

And since he asks, he learns the name of God, by which God is to be remembered, a name related to the word *to be* or *to become,* that in this book is rendered as Yahweh.

The history of the exeunt from Egypt and the entrance into the land is put in a nutshell by the poet of Psalm 114. This poem also reflects the sanctuary in Judah in the south and all Israel as parable. Notice the creation theme too in verse 7.

PSALM 114

Psalm 114 and its music is a critical test for a deciphering key. It appears that both Gregorian and Anglican chant reflect the ancient melody through the tune called by the name *tonus peregrinus*, the wandering tone.

The Song in the Night

In e-xi-tu Is-ra-el de Ae gyp to, do-mus Ja-cob de po-pu-lo bar-bar-ro.

Figure 7 Tonus peregrinus plainsong

A characteristic of this tone is the change in reciting note between the two halves of a verse, hence the term, *wandering*. We have seen how the characteristic of Haïk-Vantoura's key is to respect more than one reciting note. Even the tune in the Canadian Psalter, 1963 for Psalm 114 retains a similar movement.

"When Israel came out of Egypt, the house of Jacob from a people of strange speech."

Figure 8 Tonus peregrinus Anglican chant

The accents can also show relationships between chapters. It is evident from manuscripts among the Dead Sea scrolls that Psalm 114 and 115 were considered a pair (Yarchin :775). Psalm 115 has a unique beginning: C f#. The full pattern is shared only with Job 38.41. These two notes are shared by 21 verses as their first two notes.

PSALM 115

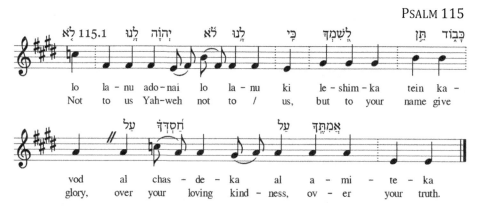

lo la-nu ado-nai lo la-nu ki le-shim-ka tein ka-
Not to us Yah-weh not to / us, but to your name give

vod al chas-de-ka al a-mi-te-ka
glory, over your loving kind-ness, ov-er your truth.

A verse with identical shape in Job.

JOB 38

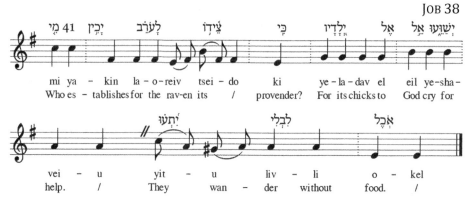

mi ya-kin la-o-reiv tsei-do ki ye-la-dav el eil ye-sha-
Who es-tablishes for the rav-en its / provender? For its chicks to God cry for

vei-u yit-u liv-li o-kel
help. / They wan-der without food. /

The exit from Egypt via the sea is celebrated in the Song of the Sea.

EXODUS 15

Sanctuary

I will make him a home, says the poet. Early in the Exodus story there is a long section on the making of the tabernacle, a place requested by Yahweh so that he could dwell among the people.

EXODUS 25

There are many distractions in the study of the Bible. The atonement is not one of them. It is curious that the English had to invent a word *at-one-ment* for it.

There is an 'at one' verse that is of central importance. It is called the Shema.

DEUTERONOMY 6

she - ma yis - ra - eil ado - nai e - lo - hei - nu ado - nai e - chad
Hear / Is - ra - el, Yah - weh is our God / Yah - weh is one.

The thought is found again, in a somewhat strange form, in the prophet Zechariah.

ZECHARIAH 14

ve - ha - yah ado - nai le - me-lek al kol ha - a - rets ba -
And it will be that Yah - weh will reign ov - er all the earth. / In

yom ha - hu yih - yeh ado - nai e - chad ush - mo e - chad
that / day it will be that Yah - weh is one and his name one.

Clearly, in this desire to be with the people, a major issue of Oneness is part of the mix. Later (see below under Servant), we will sing through the 4th servant song. Oneness does not appear to be complete in human history. My understanding, as I construct this book, is alternatively depressing and elating. Expressing such understanding is very difficult. Do we look for an enforced oneness, such as is threatened by 'the one ring' in the Lord of the Rings? Or in certain historical aspects of Christendom? Our traditions do not recommend themselves, for the expression of theories of atonement has often been with extreme violence causing division, hardly the stuff of being at-one.

EXODUS 25

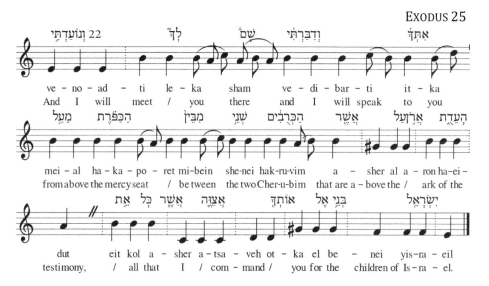

ve - no - ad - ti le - ka sham ve - di - bar - ti it - ka
And I will meet / you there and I will speak to you

mei - al ha - ka - po - ret mi-bein she-nei hak-ru-vim a - sher al a - ron ha-ei -
from above the mercy seat / between the two Cher-u-bim that are a - bove the / ark of the

dut eit kol a - sher a - tsa - veh ot - ka el be - nei yis-ra - eil
testimony, / all that I / com - mand / you for the children of Is - ra - el.

Returning to Exodus, the place where God will meet with Moses (the singular you who is addressed in the passage), is in the tabernacle in front of the mercy seat that covers the ark. The word *atonement* is a rendering of the homonym כפר, a word that also means lion, whence the pun *the Lion of Judah* (here translated as cub).

HOSEA 5

In the fundamental sense kfr means *to cover*. The English *cover* sounds like כפר. It is a very rich word in the Hebrew Bible. The Greek in the earliest translation of the Bible is rendered as ἱλαστήριον (hilasterion) the *mercy seat*, כפרת (keferet) in Hebrew, the same word as *cover* in a different form.

The Greek appears in the New Testament in Hebrews 9.5 with the gloss *mercy seat*, and in Romans 3.25 (King James Version) as *propitiation*, a widely ranging religious concept suggesting ideas related to payment, appeasement, and reconciliation. There are many facets of atonement. The whole is not revealed through only one of them. Yahweh meets with Moses at the place of mercy. In the story, this place of atonement finds its home in the temple, and in the city where Yahweh will place his name. We will come back to this in Chapter 4.

Wandering

There are many times and conditions of trouble. Some trouble happens immediately in the canonical story, and some happens after the building of the sanctuary, and during the wandering in the desert, and in the promised land before and after the exile. Right after the celebration of the crossing of the sea of reeds, there is a water problem.

EXODUS 15

Note that *bitter* should not be placed on the subdominant. The literal word order is not *They were bitter*, but *bitter were they*. *They* refers back to the plural water(s), always plural in Hebrew. But pause to consider if the reference is ambiguous.

The Song in the Night

And again soon after that at another place, they grumble again, this time against Moses and Aaron, because they are hungry.

EXODUS 16

The people have not come into their rest here. So there is no rest in those grumbling verses.

And what rest there is in verse 3 is the remembered *satiation* by the flesh-pots of the world, (that is Egypt).

Moses strongly complains to Yahweh because of the recalcitrance of the people.

NUMBERS 11

Note *ground* is אדמה. It is neither *land* nor *earth* (both these glosses are used for ארץ). To make a long story short, the children of Israel are in the wilderness for 40 years, a generation, as Psalm 95 notes.

PSALM 95

And in this psalm, *anger* is highlighted mid-verse and Yahweh swears that they will not *come into his rest* either. Note too that they *wander in their hearts*. The wilderness could well be metaphor for the difficult nature that humans exhibit in their growing up.

What is Yahweh's rest? A curious question worth holding on to. Coming into rest, as if it indicated the entry into the land, is still far from a surety. In Deuteronomy 8, situated in narrative time near the time of entry into the land, a warning is given concerning future behaviour. Here we hear the voice of Yahweh pleading for the obedience that comes with faithfulness.

Deuteronomy 8 is a standard part of the lectionary (Year A Thanksgiving). The chosen lesson begins in the middle of the recitation. (See Appendix 1 for the full lesson.) This is clear from both grammar and music, beginning at verse 6. Hear the tone of both gift and encouragement to respond and not the tone that will be common in a reading if it is read as a dire warning. It is Yahweh *aching*, if our imagination will allow, for his child.

Kugel (1981 :144) writes that the accents sometimes seem to interfere with the parallels, but his examples with the accents interpreted as music seem quite fine. The parallels are rhetorical and useful and they are clear within the musical phrases. The music will allow parallels to be heard.[11]

NUMBERS 23

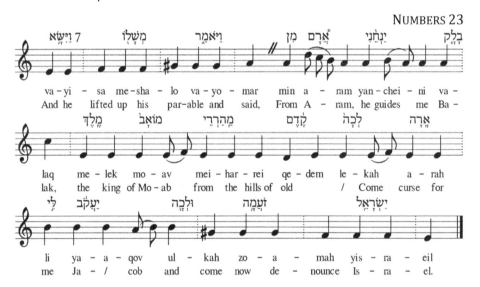

In the story, Balaam does anything but curse Israel and Balak is furious. Balaam's conversation with his donkey is music like any other conversation. Balaam is caught between a rock and a hard place and his donkey, seeing the problem, refuses repeatedly to carry him. If we could say that Israel's entry into the land is filled with

---

[11] The parallel Kugel is concerned about is *from Aram* [a], *he guides me* [b], *Balak* [c], *the king of Moab* [c'] [b' implied], *from the hills of old* [a']. It is a circular structure, but a small part of the whole, and the accents sharply point it out. I suspect, he would have ignored the silluq since it is in the middle and not the end of the verse, and so out of place for such an important accent (it is an emperor).

prophetic promise, we could also say that the human is filled with conflict and this is reflected in the contrary messages in this passage.

NUMBERS 22

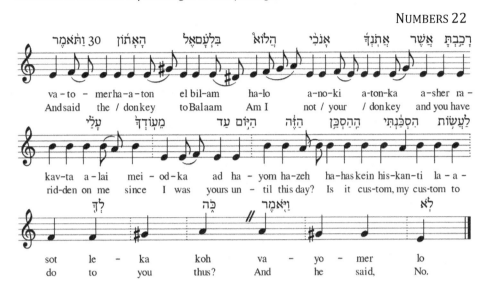

Balaam gets to the place of his parable and blesses with open eyes the tents of the people of this canonical story.

NUMBERS 24

His words are reflected in Psalm 84. This juxtaposition reflects the desire of God, even in the conflict evident and absorbed by the poor she-donkey, to live with the people.

PSALM 84

Instruction

Wickes writes concerning the Decalogue (in Exodus 20 and Deuteronomy 5) that the two sets come from the Orientals and Occidentals "breaking up the longer verses and bringing together the shorter ones. (1887 :131). Others have the tradition, e.g. the anonymous text in Figure 9 (1744 :41), that the two sets of te'amim reflect two reading modes, one to be used in synagogue, and one for study. The reading in synagogue splits the Decalogue more obviously into 10 distinct utterances, and so necessitates a different set of te'amim of accommodate the different lexical parsing.

N the two Tables of the Duplicate Verſions of the Decalogue, (wherein the Words in different Charaſter repreſent thoſe in the *Hebrew* that are doubly accented) the firſt Paſuch or Paragraph of the firſt Column in each Table, is divided into three Parts by abſolute Lords ; *viz.* by two Colons ; the firſt made by the abſolute King in Proſe, and the ſecond by the Emperor *Athnach* ; and cloſed with a Period, by the Emperor *Silluk* : But in the ſecond Column of each Table, the ſame is divided into five Verſes, or Silluks of the Law ; as may alſo

Figure 9 Accents as kings, lords, emperors

The music proposed by Haïk-Vantoura has no difficulty in accepting multiple notes per syllable. The second note becomes the reciting note. Here are four short verses from the Decalogue in Exodus in what is effectively E minor. Note that there are no rest points in any of these verses.

(I could have glossed *associate* as *friend* or even *shepherd*. They are all the same three letters. See below under Commandment on Leviticus 19.18.)

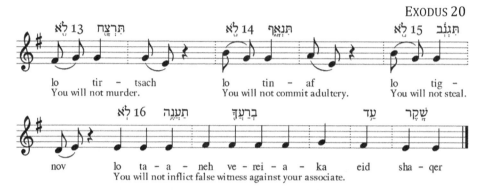

EXODUS 20

lo tir - tsach
You will not murder.

lo tin - af
You will not commit adultery.

lo tig -
You will not steal.

nov lo ta - a - neh ve - rei - a - ka eid sha - qer
You will not inflict false witness against your associate.

There are many possible modes. It is worth noting that there are some aspects of traditional cantillation, the slurred descending fourths and fifths, that are similar to what we hear with the multiple reciting notes on a single syllable.

The Lydian mode (effectively E major but without explicit use of the leading tone) makes this passage easier to sing by avoiding the augmented fourth.

a - no - ki adon - nai e - lo - hei - ka a - sher ho - tsei - ti - ka mei -
I / am Yah weh / your God who brought you / forth from the

e - rets mits - rai - yim mi - beit a - va - dim
land of / Egypt out of the house / of serv - itude.

The Decalogue in Deuteronomy 5 is addressed to a new generation. Notice the present tense in verse 3 and the repeated phrasing of the same present and personal address. As with atonement, the subject of being present to the time of the commandment as if it were in our own day, is a subject to which much careful study can be given. Without going into detail, this making present the past is the essence of remembering.

Why are there two sets of accents? The Decalogue is by no means the only book where two reciting-note accents can appear on one syllable. But in the Decalogue, there is a density of these accents that is specific to the two locations. Perhaps it could be suggested that the subject of the Decalogue invites a more detailed music, that it should be highlighted because of the importance of the Instruction. While some may see Law as opposed to grace and say they depend solely on grace, such a comment risks its foundation. It is one reason I use *Instruction* rather than *Law* for *Torah*. For who would want to live without instruction from God, in whatever name such a one is known?

DEUTERONOMY 5

The second time, the music is different. (Compare Deuteronomy 5.6 with Exodus 20.2) There is no rest in verse 6 below as there is in the corresponding verse 2 in Exodus. The Aleppo codex is not available for this chapter to verify the data from the Leningrad codex.

The singular nature of the commandment is highlighted in verse 31. Yahweh addresses Moses:

The commandment is one rather than many. This will be particularly evident in the foundation statement of the unity of Yahweh God, *Hear O Israel*.

Commandment

DEUTERONOMY 6

The one commandment that follows this statement of the unity of Yahweh is the great commandment.

All your *might* is the traditional gloss. Nothing held back, With every fibre of your being, as my Hebrew coach explained to me. The other great commandment is from Leviticus. This second of the summary of the Torah, being like the first commandment, we could say, it is also at one with it: *You will love your associate as yourself.*

LEVITICUS 19

ta – le – rei – a – ka   ka – mo – ka   a – ni   ado – nai
love your / as – sociate as your – self. / I   am   Yah – weh.

Associate is an odd gloss for this famous passage. The word is רעה,[12] a word with a range of glosses: *friend*, *shepherd*, or *fellow*. *Neighbour*, where I use it, is the root שכן, the same root as *dwell*. I have chosen *neighbour* as one who lives near us or dwells nearby, rather than the more general sense of one's fellow creature, whether physically near or on the other side of the world via electronic communications.

A long agreement is embodied in the music of Deuteronomy chapter 28. When we come to this passage we have come full circle in this book back to the story of Job. Job suffers several of the curses of Deuteronomy 28. This clear allusion in Job to the text of the treaty between Yahweh and Israel shows us that the play is a working out of the false implications of these curses. What are the true implications? In a word, as an early teacher of mine, Peter Craigie, said: Deuteronomy is a book of love in spite of the warnings. The warnings are over the top in this chapter. It is written for a very jealous lover.

DEUTERONOMY 28

ve – ha – yah ka – a – sher sas   ado – nai   a – lei – kem   le – hei –
And it will hap – pen that as Yah – weh sang for joy ov – er you   to /

tiv et – kem   ul – har – bot et – kem   kein   ya – sis ado – nai   a – lei – kem   le – ha – a –
do for you   good and to make you   increase so Yah – weh will sing for joy over you   to make you

vid   et – kem ul – hash – mid   et – kem   ve – ni – sach – tem   mei – al
perish /   and to ex – ter – minate   you,   and you /   will be   plucked

ha – a – da – mah   a – sher   a – tah va   sha – mah   le – rish – tah
from the   . ground that you are   going to – ward to /   pos – sess it.

Deuteronomy 28 is traditionally translated with God cursing, but it is not about God cursing the people or anything else, it is about the people denying God as revealed to them in the words of Moses. And it foresees exile. This is not a book on historical criticism, but one can see the text as revealing a growth in the understanding of the writers based on new historical conditions. The chanting itself will arise out of a desire to tell the story again after many years of composition and reflection.

---

[12] See Chapter 7 for a full list of Hebrew letters. For the most part I will not transcribe the letters in the text since they are all transcribed in the music.

4. Home

I have heard it said that the church, now in the wilderness, is on a journey to the promised land. This is a limited use of the metaphor. The 'church' is also home, also in exile, and also restored. The Church is also in Egypt, a guest in an alien land, and wandering in the wilderness. *Church* is too limited a term, as if the down and up experience did not apply to peoples, congregations, assemblies, and even individuals in all traditions.

Earth

The entry into the land across the Jordan is piecemeal and complex. The land is full of enemies and troubles from tribal warfare to personal jealousies. If this is the promised land, we find that there is war in this heaven. Leaders come and go. In the period of the Judges,

JUDGES 17

This verse is repeated as the last verse of Judges with identical music. Deuteronomy includes a similar phrase in chapter 12, verse 8, as if to say that the situation we find in the time of the Judges is not acceptable to the writer of Deuteronomy.

DEUTERONOMY 12

How does a social structure work when there is no leadership that incorporates the people? Leadership may not incorporate what is good for all. The record of the kings that do arise in Israel is only occasionally a cause for praise.

Passing over the book of Judges, we come to the book named after the last judge before the monarchy, Samuel. Samuel is a just judge, who never took so much as a donkey from anyone.

1 SAMUEL 12

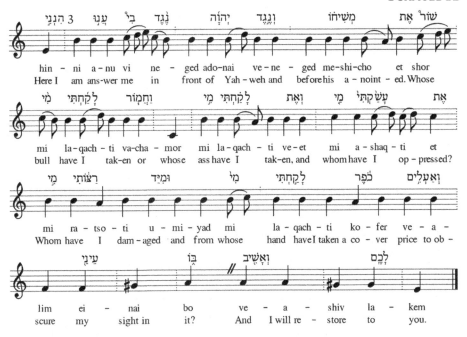

Note the repeated ornamentation in the first and second sentences. This sequence (qarne, pashta, geresh) occurs in 1280 verses. Perhaps it is indicative of a raised voice.

Samuel is the child Hannah prayed for in her barrenness. Her song after his birth anticipates the Magnificat of Luke's gospel (beginning at Luke 1.46).

1 SAMUEL 2

Samuel, though still in his youth, hears the condemnation of the sons of Eli and the priesthood of the religious establishment of the time. Those we call children understand perfectly well what is good.

1 SAMUEL 3

The books of Samuel cover the stories of David, the youngest son of Jesse. One all time famous if not favorite story is the David and Goliath sequence.

This sequence, in the lectionary for Year B, the season after Pentecost, is a dramatic passage requiring a narrator, a Saul, a David, and a Philistine. The first passage is a dialogue between Saul and David. The second between Saul and the Philistine. If you have only three voices, Saul and the Philistine may be played by one voice. Just have Saul move to the other side of David for the second scene. This has been performed unaccompanied as a lesson. (We didn't skip any of the verses.) It really gets people's attention. The Old Testament lesson is no longer the same old same old. Here are two of the verses to note the ornaments around the weapons in the beginning of verse 39 and the middle of verse 40. (See Appendix 1 for the full score of the lesson.) These are the only words so ornamented in the text of the passage.

1 SAMUEL 17

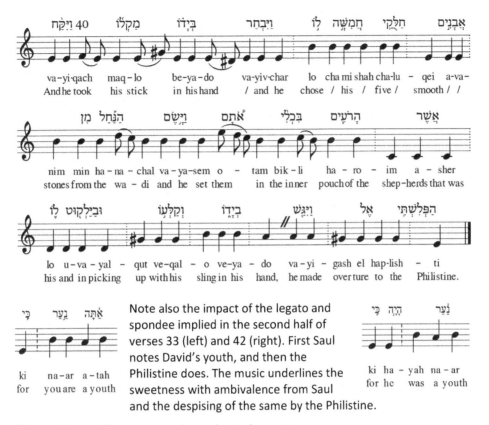

Note also the impact of the legato and spondee implied in the second half of verses 33 (left) and 42 (right). First Saul notes David's youth, and then the Philistine does. The music underlines the sweetness with ambivalence from Saul and the despising of the same by the Philistine.

This musical motif appears nowhere else in the section.

Monarchy

The Biblical story does not paper over the failures of the kings of Israel or Judah. They are all tarnished. David with Bathsheba, Solomon in the accession to his throne, and the rest of them failing with few exceptions. The child Josiah, one of the last kings of Jerusalem, is remembered for his example.

2 CHRONICLES 34

In this passage we see that king David is remembered as a model.

From the point of view of music, David is a great king. He brought the ark into Jerusalem and housed it in a tent. The service before this ark is recounted in 1 Chronicles 16. Three psalms are sung. This makes it possible to compare the psalms as they are in the Psalter with three examples pointed with the prose accents. As we noted under 2 Samuel 22 (which parallels Psalm 18), the words and the versification may be different, as well as the music.

Before the psalms are sung, the generosity of the king is noted. He begins the praises with the choir and its head that he appointed from the Levites. This verse (measure 6) has the interesting feature of the list of people split by the pazer (ב֤) accent as if it were a comma delimiting the list and yet with great additional variety also.

1 CHRONICLES 16

The repetition of psalm texts in 1 Chronicles illustrates the use of prose accents in imitation of the poetic and in this case with a stronger alignment to the sentence structure. 1 Chronicles 16.8 has accents that encourage reading it as a tri-colon. The equivalent Psalm verse (105.1, see Chapter 6 below) is a bi-colon separated by the atnah. The music of each set of accents can effectively divide the line. The atnah seldom occurs in this chapter. In verses 7 to 33, it occurs only in verses 29 and 33. This is in contrast to its use in the Psalter in these same poems.

shi - ru la - ado - nai kol ha - a - rets bas - ru mi - yom el yom ye - shu - a -
Sing to Yahweh all the earth. Publish from day to day his salvation.

to sap - ru va - go - yim et ke - vo - do be - kol ha - a - mim nif - le - o -
Recount in the nations his glory, to all the peoples his wonders.

tav ki ga - dol ado - nai um - hu - lal me - od ve - no - ra hu al kol e - lo -
For great is Yahweh and much to be praised. He is to be feared above all gods.

him ki kol e - lo - hei ha - a - mim e - li lim va ado - nai sha - mai yim a - sah
For all the gods of the peoples are good for nothing, but Yahweh made the heavens.

hod ve - ha - dar le - fa - nav oz ve - ched - vah bim - qo -
Splendour and honour are in his presence. Strength and cheer are in his place.

mo ha - vu la - ado - nai mish pe - chot a - mim ha - vu la - ado - nai ka - vod va -
Ascribe to Yahweh families of the peoples, ascribe to Yahweh glory and strength.

oz ha - vu la - ado - nai ke - vod she - mo se - u min - chah u -
Ascribe to Yahweh the glory of his name. Bear a gift and come into his presence.

vo - u le - fa - nav hish - ta - cha - vu la - ado - nai be - had - rat qo - desh
Worship Yahweh in the honour of holiness.

chi - lu mil - fa - naiv kol ha - a - rets af ti - kon tei - veil bal ti -
Let all the earth be brought to birth from his presence. Indeed the world is established so it will not move.

mot yis me – chu ha-sha-mai – yim ve-ta – geil ha-a-rets ve yom – ru va-go – yim ado-

Let the heavens be glad and let the earth rejoice, and let them say in the nations, Yahweh reigns.

nai ma – lak   yir – am ha yam   um-lo-o ya-a – lots ha-sa – deh ve-kol a-sher   bo

Let the sea thunder and its fullness, let the field be elated and all that are in it.

az ye ran – nu a – tsei ha – ya-ar mi lif – nei adonai   ki   va lish – pot et ha – a–rets

Then the trees of the wood will shout for joy from the presence of Yahweh, for he comes to judge the earth.

Psalm 96, the middle of the three psalms of 1 Chronicles 16, is the first of a group of four psalms in Book 4 that extol Yahweh as monarch. It has a particularly striking musical form. Verses 4, 5, 10 and 13 all have the highest reciting note and ornaments and each one expresses security in the judgment of the world by the one who made it. The music is in Appendix 1. The psalm is the Lectionary psalm for Christmas.

Comparison with 1 Chronicles 16.23-33 above shows that the music is different. Verses 23 to 28, 30-32 chant on the high C and move to the tonic without a rest. Pauses are conveyed by the ornaments rather than the major rest of the atnah. The paragraph structure is different.

1 Chronicles 16.8-36 from the Letteris edition shows a number of additional meteg accents (=silluq) which are varied from both the Aleppo and the Leningrad codices. Levin

Figure 10 The Aleppo codex, Psalm 96.1

(1994 :129) notes a tendency that earlier manuscripts have fewer meteg accents but here both Aleppo and Leningrad are also different. While the differences are not critical to transparency, they do make one wonder what the rationale was in the scribe's mind for the additional accents. Were they accents for reading only? I suspect so. But if followed as music, they frequently bring the music down from a C recitation to a low e recitation. As a result, verses that would have had a similar shape in the song now differ.

Some changes are also evident between later editions of Psalm 96. Letteris has added a meteg and again, likely inadvertently, changed the music. Letteris 1946 was not aware of Haïk-Vantoura's work. The meteg may have been deemed necessary for stress but is not needed for the music, and this particular one (Figure 10) is not in the Aleppo or the Leningrad codex. But it sounds very rhythmic and suitable in the context. This demonstrates that the text as we have received it may have copying problems that impair or enhance, even if by accident, the effectiveness of the music derived according to Haïk-Vantoura's key. Note the three part final verse with the cadence (ole-veyored) on the second, at the word *earth*.

1 Chronicles 16

ve im ru   hoshi ei - nu   e-lo - hei yishei-nu veqab - tsei nu ve ha tsi - lei-nu minha-go-

And say, Save us, O God of our salvation, and collect us and deliver us from the nations,

yim   le-ho-dot   le - sheim qad-she-ka   le-hish-ta - bei-ach bit-hi-la - te-ka

to give thanks to your holy name, to commend your praises.

Here is another example of the same words set to two differing sets of accents. 1 Chronicles 16.35 above and Psalm 106.47 below.

Psalm 106

ho-shi-ei - nu ado - nai e-lo-hei - nu ve-qab tsei-nu   min ha-go - yim

Save us Yahweh our God, and collect us from the nations,

le-ho-dot le - sheim qad - she-ka   le - hish-ta-bei - ach bit-hi-la - te-ka

to give thanks to your holy name,   to commend your praises.

David is a great and beloved king, poet, and musician. His final words are given the status of oracles.

2 Samuel 23

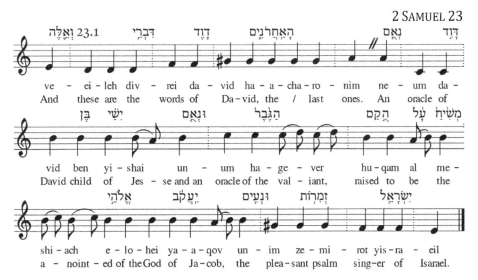

ve - ei - leh div - rei da - vid ha-a-cha-ro - nim   ne - um da -

And these are the words of Da-vid, the / last ones. An oracle of

vid ben yi-shai   un - um ha-ge - ver   hu - qam al me -

David child of Jes - se and an oracle of the val - iant,   raised to be the

shi - ach   e - lo - hei ya-a-qov un - im ze-mi - rot yis-ra - eil

a - noint - ed of the God of Ja-cob, the plea-sant psalm sing-er of Isarael.

The rebuke of the prophet Nathan over his adultery with Bathsheba and his murder of Uriah casts a long shadow over his anointed reign.

2 SAMUEL 12

David's example is made public in the sight of the sun, to billions of people through the commentary of Psalm 51. This is David's admission that God is right. What we do has consequences.

While most readers read this psalm as one of repentance, each section of the psalm has a central word related to *righteousness*, the righteousness of the Other. The word for *righteousness* appears in this verse and in verses 16 and the final verse 21. These are the only verses in this psalm with a reciting note on the sixth. The verbal structure and the musical structure reinforce each other.

PSALM 51

David sins against God in the woman and God in the Hittite.

The prophecy of Nathan finds its fulfillment in Absalom's rebellion. Perhaps the most telling musical miniature of David is his lament over this beloved son, Absalom.

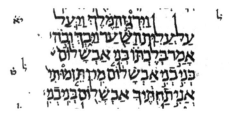

Figure 11 Part of the Leningrad Codex, 2 Samuel 19.1

41

2 SAMUEL 19

Moving on from the king whose name is beloved to the one whose name means peace and who is in the inscription of 2 psalms (72, the last psalm in Book 3, and 127, the middle psalm of the Psalms of Ascent) as opposed to David's 75 (or 76 if you count Psalm 10).

PSALM 72

Solomon's ills get blamed on his wives. And David's sins are forgotten in the comparison. But perhaps implicitly, it is their old age that is compared, and the one whose name is peace is not at peace, but the one whose name is beloved somehow finds rest even having not built the house he wanted to build.

1 KINGS 11

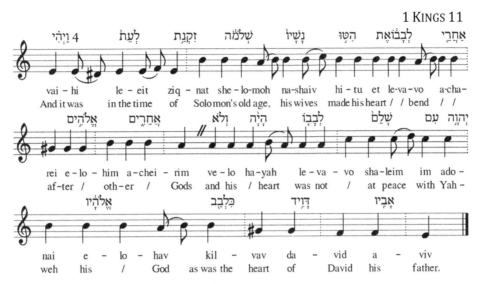

They are both beloved. And between them, David planned and Solomon built the temple (the house for my name) that David was not allowed to build.

1 CHRONICLES 28

The house for the divine Name is the place where the ark, and its cover with the cherubim over the mercy seat, will come to rest. It comes into the temple with great fanfare.

PSALM 24

The ark combines the mercy-seat and the Decalogue.

1 KINGS 8

ein ba-a-ron raq she-nei lu-chot ha-a-va-nim a-sher hi-ni-ach
There was nothing in the ark but the two / tab-lets of / stone / that / Mo-ses

sham mo-sheh be-cho-reiv a-sher ka-rat ado-nai im be-
left / there in / Horeb, / which Yah-weh / cut with the

nei yis-ra-eil be-tsei-tam mei — e-rets mits-ra-yim
children of Isra-el at their going out from the land / of Egy-pt.

And it is king Solomon, the child of the house of David, who provides the house for the ark. And when the ark entered that house, though itself small and practically empty, there was no room for the priests to enter.

2 CHRONICLES 7

ve — lo yak-lu ha-ko-ha-nim la-vo el beit ado-nai ki ma-
And the priests were not able to en-ter in — to the house of Yah-weh, for the

lei ke-vod ado-nai et beit ado-nai
glo-ry of Yah-weh had filled the house of Yah-weh.

1 KINGS 9

va-yo-mer ado-nai ei-lav sha-ma-ti et te-fi-lat-
And Yah-weh / said to him, I have heard your prayer and your

ka ve-et te-chi-nat-ka a-sher hit-cha-nan-tah le-fa-na hiq-dash-ti et ha-
sup-pli-ca-tion / that you have gracious-ly made to / my face. / I have sanc-ti-

bai – yit ha – zeh a – sher ba – ni – tah la – sum she – mi sham ad o –
fi – ed this house that you have built / to put my name there for ever –

lam ve – ha – yu ei – nai ve – li – bi sham kol ha – ya – mim
more. And my eyes / and my / heart will be there eve – ry day.

You will frequently find very long recitations on the B as in this passage with many syllables without accent, but the whole leading to a cadence, or an accent that is effectively a comma.

The coronation of Solomon is celebrated every time a British sovereign is crowned since the time of Handel through the coronation anthem, *Zadok the Priest*. Solomon's heritage has lasted, though one usually forgets the political assassinations that happened just after his anointing.

1 KINGS 1

va – yi – qach tsa doq ha – ko – hein et qe – ren ha – she – men min ha – o – hel va yim –
And he took Za dok the / priest the horn of / oil from the tent and he an –

shach et she – lo – moh va – yit – qe – u ba – sho – far va –
noint – ed / / Solomon. And they sound – ed the sho – far and

yo – me – ru kol ha – am ye – chi ha – me – lek she – lo – moh
all the peo – ple / said / May the king, Sol – o – mon live.

Riddle

The Hebrew Bible is not without riddle or parable.

PSALM 49

a – teh le – ma – shal az – ni ef – tach be – ki – nor chi – da – ti
I will bend to a parable my ear. I will open on a harp / my riddle.

The Psalms are a comprehensive commentary on the Hebrew Bible. They are far and away the most popular of the books of the Old Testament. Their purpose is to form and preserve a people that learns and administers mercy. It's not surprising that all the way through the creation of this book, psalms spring to mind to keep the threads together.

Within the writings, I have already introduced Job, the mega-parable. The narrator repeatedly refers to Job's speech as *parable,* as does Job himself in his wrap-up.

JOB 30

So, in short, we are to read the ancient texts figuratively, whatever history they imply. (There are many distractions in the study of the Bible.)

Another book in the writings is Qohelet, also known as Ecclesiastes. Here is the famous section on time, chapter 3. You can see how the verses are all connected together, verses 3 to 8 all beginning on the high C as if they were all completing a single thought. Where is the rest, the atnah, in this passage? Imagine composing this passage.

QOHELET 3

Now it is time to look at the book of Proverbs, poetry like the Psalms. The short crisp rhythms are clear from syllable counts, and from the use of the poetic accents. This is true whether we look at the first 8 chapters or the many chapters of less connected aphorisms.

PROVERBS 9

Proverbs 2 reveals another example of connections between verses through the accents. The first unusual note in the music is verse 1 which begins on the third rather than on the tonic.

PROVERBS 2

This instruction does not start from scratch, but implicitly connects with the prior chapter. Then verse 3 highlights the strong conditional by beginning with a high C.

The Song in the Night

Verse 4 is extremely simple E-F#-A rest A-F#-E return.

im te-vaq – she-nah ka – ka-sef   ve-ka-mat-mo – nim tach-pe – se-nah
If you /   seek her as   sil-ver,   and as buried, you in – ves – ti-gate   her. /

Verse 5 highlights the consequence seeking wisdom with an ornament on *then*.

az   ta-vin yir – at ado – nai   ve – da-at e-lo – him tim – tsa
then   you will discern the   fear of Yah – weh,   and know ledge / of God you will   find.

Note the recurrence of *then* in verse 9, highlighted with a similar ornament.

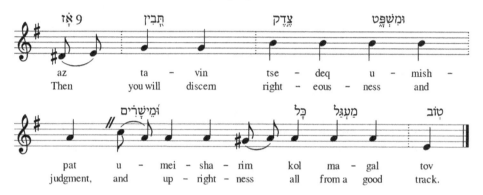

az   ta – vin   tse – deq   u – mish –
Then   you will   discern   right – eous – ness   and

pat   u – mei – sha – rim   kol   ma – gal   tov
judgment,   and   up – right – ness   all   from a   good   track.

Verses 11 to 15 are the first half of a long sentence stretching to the end of the
chapter and begun by verse 11, which has two hopes: to deliver from evil (12-15) and
to deliver from the strange woman (16-19). Verse 11 shows its uniqueness in the set
as the only verse without a mid-verse rest.

me – zi – mah tish – mor   a – lei – ka   te – vu – nah tin – tse – re – kah
In – ten – tion will   guard be – side   you   and discern ment will pre – serve-you.

leha – tsil-ka mi-de – rek   ra   mei – ish me – da – beir tah-pu – kot
tode – liver you from the way of   evil,   from a per – son speaking changeable / things.

ha – oz-vim ar – chot   yo-sher   la – le – ket be-dar-kei   cho-shek
(Those who for – sake the paths of the   upright   to   walk   in the ways of   darkness,

Verses 11, 12, and 13, and 14 all begin on the third, showing the continuing first part of the sentence. Finally verse 15 begins and ends on the tonic. Then verses 16 and 17 begin on the third and verse 18 again highlights the ki with the high C.

Verse 19 closes this second hope with a verse beginning and ending on the tonic, and the final two verses reflect the ultimate consequence of the long conditional of the chapter, repeating the ornament that was on *then* (אז) on the *in order that* (לְמַעַן) that begins verse 20. There appear to be multiple threads in this sentence, so I have included some parentheses.

PROVERBS 8

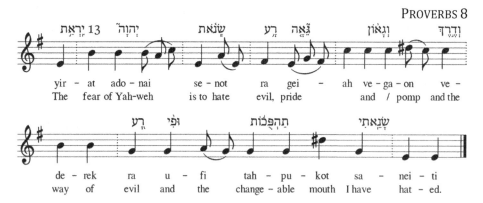

Chapter 8, verse 13 is striking in its word painting. It is a bi-colon with the only rest in the verse on the supertonic. The word *changeable* on the stark ornament in the Hebrew could be rendered *delinquent*. Haïk-Vantoura has little to go on in selecting the meaning of ornaments. This one she chose as the leap of a fifth up (or a fourth down if the former is too high) because of its similarity to the fifth from the tonic that this sign represents below the letters. This might be considered unmusical but it is certainly striking word-painting in this and other cases (e.g. Psalm 4 noted in Chapter 7).

Verse 23 in this chapter has no rest, a continuous sacrifice from the beginning for the life of the world.

Sometimes when I consider my choice of glosses, I cannot remember why I chose a particular gloss. The root here is קדם. It has a number of choices in my data: *confront, prior, antiquity, old, stalled, preceding, east, go before*. I have allowed myself choice but refused just to pick a gloss that makes sense to me if it conflicts with glosses already chosen. Of course, one could imagine a scribal error and postulate a different stem like קצה *extremities*, or אפס *ends*. I have left this piece of the puzzle as above for now.

Verse 30 is a tri-colon.

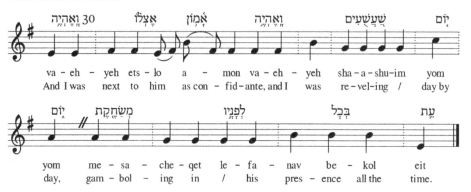

The interval on *day by day* C to A is rare. In 1 Kings 6.2, the interval sings *its breadth*, of the house that King Solomon built for Yahweh. In Psalm 137.7, the words are *raze, raze*. Other than those two instances, the interval only occurs in Proverbs 6.3 (*for you come into the palm of your friend*), this verse, 8.30, and 8.34 (again *day by day*). In Proverbs 8 it finds a definitive echo. The building of the house for Yahweh, the ultra-violence of Psalm 137, and the betrayal of a friend, perhaps these also are day by day experiences.

And Verse 33 has no significant rest. It could have had one on *wise*. Why not? Perhaps the revia is sufficient, but sing straight on.

The word *parable* or *riddle* is not in the Song, but it has its analogical interpretation. Traditionally ascribed to Solomon, the opening voice is a female voice. Filled with imagery, all are encouraged to read it taking the female role.

SONG 1

There is no mention of Yahweh in the Song but suggestive names are hidden in the sounds of the animals in the repeated refrain.

SONG 2

The Song in the Night

The Psalms are equally familiar with the love motif.

ye - e - rav a-lav si - chi a - no-ki es - mach ba-ado - nai
Sweet on him is / my pondering, I my-self will be glad in Yah - weh.

5. Exile

Protest

No one should take on the prophets with such few strokes. But this is a limited sketch.

It is not as if the people of the time of the later prophets were somehow more sinful than the people of an earlier time that they deserved such a great prophet as Isaiah. There is plenty of sin to go around in all ages. But here we have the grief that the sin causes highlighted in a particular way.[13]

ISAIAH 1

The prophet undoes the religion of the cult. We haven't said enough about the desire of the human to approach the holy. It is a serious theme in both the Old and New Testaments. Knowing about it is not the same as being enabled to do it. Doing it is a matter of turning and approaching. Leviticus requires a blood sacrifice. Suffice it to say that the regulations of the cult are a well-established and well-controlled religious process with all the baggage that goes with such an establishment including the very strong tendencies of abuse of power and the problems of surface compliance. Remember the call of Samuel (see Chapter 4 above).

In the sacrifice of an animal, the blood symbolizes the gift of the life of the person who is approaching and offering the gift. The animal's death takes the place of the death of the offeror. But it is not the blood of goats that is needed. It is the blood of the person approaching. Clearly this is a dead end if all the offeror's blood is required.

---

[13] Kugel (1981 :111) claims the g# as a necessary accent to include the words any more in the first question rather than as a modifier for the second sentence. Comparing verse 5 with verse 2, however, shows that such an inference from this accent is not justified.

SoSoSoSoSo

LEVITICUS 1

So the animal is the substitute. Is this symbolic death strong enough to actually effect the necessary change in behaviour of the one(s) who approach? Is it sufficient to make them holy in the sight of God? If holiness includes the care of others as is illustrated in the character of the God as portrayed, then one has to assume from the evidence that the answer to this question is, No. But maybe God blinks occasionally.

Isaiah protests that God is not interested in the cult process.

ISAIAH 1

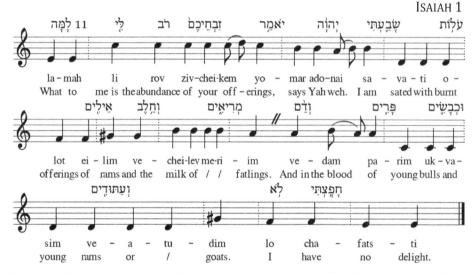

The music is not balanced with the grammar. The rest (on *fatlings*) occurs right in the middle of the list. Other translations adjust the grammar to fit. It seems to me that imbalance is just what is required. The body, the whole body of the people, individual and corporately, is out of balance and the music reflects it. There is perhaps too much pride in the fattest offering.

Isaiah is commissioned (chapter 6) in the year of the death of the king Uzziah.

ISAIAH 6

And the prophet is given a vision in the temple.

The vision of Isaiah is still sung around the world as the Sanctus. Note the descending octave in both verses 2 and 3, like the Sanctus in the B Minor Mass by Bach. This particular sequence in verse 2 to the subdominant from the octave occurs 12 times.[14]

The sequence of accents in verse 1 spelling out a descending major seventh followed by the rising sequence (B-c-d-f-g#-B-A) occurs 88 times in the prose books. In the default mode, this includes a diminished seventh chord. Smaller pieces of such a sequence are frequent. The singer needs to become adept at the tonal memory. It is foreign in some senses to us though not unheard of. It is common in Bach, but the tuning would not be equi-tempered of course. It is, in my opinion, unlike any sequence in any European music of the last five centuries that I am familiar with. I may have missed it in my singing experience, but over the last 50 years I have sung many thousands of examples. So anyone accusing Haïk-Vantoura of imitating Poulenc, or Messaien, or Gounod should produce specific examples.

---

[14] Recitation on high C followed by c-d-f-g-A, Genesis 38.21, Exodus 34.31, Leviticus 25.33, Deuteronomy 11.13, 1 Samuel 3.11, 6.6, 14.32, 24.10, 23.26, 2 Kings 14.8, Isaiah 6.2, Jeremiah 42.4. Of these 2 Kings 14.7-8 is different since verse 8 begins on the dominant rather than the tonic.

And the prophet is given a commission that is startlingly bare.

This people. Do we identify with them? In our science, we have learned that our own speech and vision can block and blind us as to what we are able to hear and see. Such internal locks are a protection mechanism. Scientists say we are living in a paradigm that we become unaware of. We need to let new evidence shake us out of it. Was exile inevitable then? If we found our vision of the peaceable kingdom, would we have to destroy it also? At both the beginning and the end of Isaiah we find such hope. The financial wolves lie down with the lamb slain on the beach, and the lions with their bombs destroyed rebuild the shattered barns of the heifer, and the subtle nakedness of the snake is satisfied with dust.

ISAIAH 65

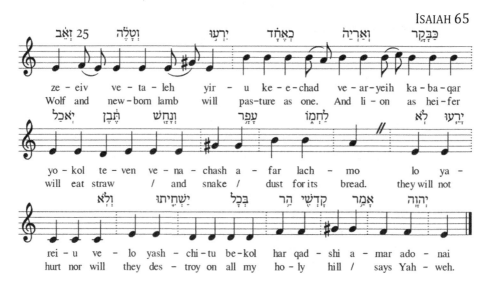

ISAIAH 2

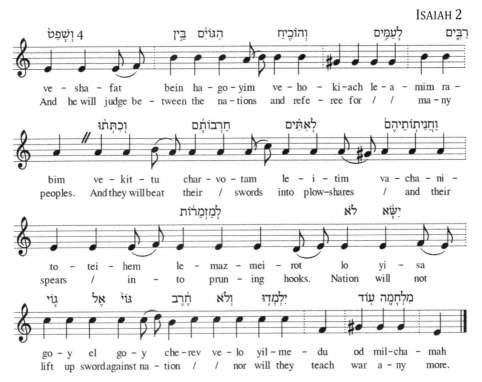

In contrast to Isaiah with the image of the peaceable kingdom, the prophet Joel tells us to *sanctify* a battle. Then he says to the vanquished, *beat your plowshares into swords.*

JOEL 4

The word for pruning hook is the same three letters as a psalm, זמר. The Psalms are sharp enough. So perhaps we could deal with our violence through singing a psalm instead.

Joel continues with the call of the nations to the valley of *Jehoshaphat*, the valley of *Yahweh-judging*. Yahweh gives judgment in favour of the weak and the homeless. God is prejudiced, a preferential option for the poor.

The Song in the Night

The first long recitation is on the tonic low E in verse 2. After the rest there is a 14-beat recitation on the subdominant, A, the note of the rest, the God of Israel pleading. Who can plead in battle from a position of rest?

Lament

The lament is prayer, face to face, honest, troubled, and open-ended. The poet asks for judgment and close advocacy with an unmerciful nation. It is a contrast with the grumbling in the desert.

PSALM 43

This is not necessarily an individual's poem. As noted above at the end of Chapter 1, Psalms 42 and 43 together are a first person singular statement of lament in exile. The mode (in the case of the Psalms, I have largely followed Haïk-Vantoura's mode choices) includes a sharpened subdominant almost precluding rest. Psalm 44 is a second lament, this time in the first person plural. Like Adam, Job, Israel (Jacob) and Jesus, whom the gospel reports as saying: *I am the vine*, the one individual poet of the Psalms embodies all. The prayer for judgment is not a self-satisfied claim, but a prayer for correction. God's judgment may be painful but will be effective.

In Psalm 74, the psalmist pleads for decisive action as if Yahweh is holding his cards close to his chest. Kugel (1981 :115) says the accents contradict the parallelism. But he interprets כלה as *remove*, whereas perhaps it is a plea that the closely held hand, even the right hand be exposed to *finish* or *consummate* victory rather than defeat, on behalf of the people. I.e. to *consume* the enemy.

PSALM 74

These laments arise out of the failure of the monarchy. The insight of Ethan the Ezrahite, is the longest lament in the Psalms. It begins with a song to Yahweh.

PSALM 89

The third person address switches to the second person. Note the shalshelet ornament. The psalmist is the I that lives *from generation to generation,* so the singer must be the body of Israel, the vine that was brought out of Egypt.

PSALM 80

Psalm 80, like the majority of the psalms in Books 2 and 3 (42-89), is also a lament. The pattern of complaint in the presence of God repeats. The complaint is real and it is directed to God. You sprung us from Egypt, why do you now destroy us?

Psalm 89 levels far more than one complaint against God. The series begins in verse 49 and continues for eight verses. Speaking of the line of the kings who are descended from David, the poet uses very strong language.

PSALM 89

One result of this breach of the fences of Judah and Israel is the ultimate lament poetry in the Lamentations of Jeremiah. The first four chapters of Lamentations are alphabetic acrostic poems.[15]

LAMENTATIONS 1

---

[15] Other acrostics in the Bible are Psalms 9-10, 25, 34, 37, in Book 1; 111, 112, 119, 145, in Book 2, and Proverbs 31. There are five psalms in Book 1 comprising four acrostics, and four in Book 5. They are strategically placed in the Psalter, each one celebrating the psalm immediately preceding it. The groups of four strongly link the Psalms to the experience of exile represented in the Lamentations. (MacDonald: 2013: 41).

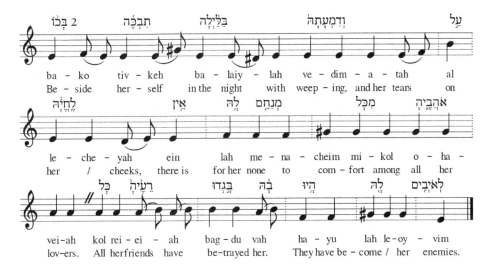

Servant

Isaiah 52-53 is the fourth of four songs in the book of the consolation of Israel (Isaiah 40 to 55).

ISAIAH 52

As with David's lament over the death of Absalom, where the music on *he went up* goes down, so here the music on *exalted* is a sudden drop to the extreme low range of the scale.

The desolation of *then* is quite like the desolation that is *now*. Who is this servant? Exploitation, poverty, and violence can close in on anyone and severe distortion will be the result. Will there be any release from such trouble, and any justice?

We are presented with a cultic image of the blood of the offering being spattered against the altar. Before we get to the cult though, we might notice that Isaiah grants to the astonished sovereigns the *seeing* and *hearing* that is denied to the people in Isaiah's commissioning vision. The statement is introduced by an elaborate ornament. This is significant since the word it is on is very common.

Now to the sacrificial imagery. Even the music of verses 14 and 15 paints the parallels we are meant to hear: the desolation of the sovereigns, the spattering of the nations, and the understanding that comes to the nations that was missed in the directed teaching to Israel. Everyone is to learn from this, not just Israel, the elder child, but the younger gentiles also who are grafted in to the promises made in the vine.

LEVITICUS 4

This word *spatter* is used mostly in Leviticus, where the cult sacrifices are detailed. Spattering occurs once more in Isaiah.

ISAIAH 63

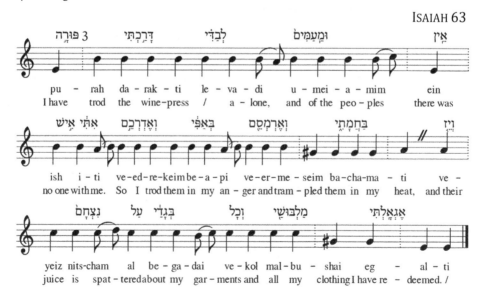

The music is a long pair of recitations on the dominant followed by a long recitation on the sixth. Redemption is related to the blood. This is an image our culture is not comfortable with. The cup of wine is a symbol of such anger, again with the exile in the background of this central poem from the Psalms.

PSALM 75

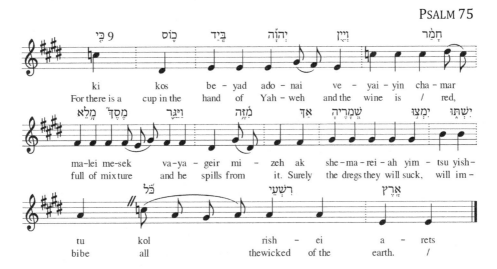

The Hebrew is striking in the vehemence of the single syllables. My translation has too many syllables. You could reduce them in performance to *For a cup, hand.* This is in a major-minor mode resulting in a downward leap of a minor seventh. The music then returns to the high note for *the wine is red* before a recitation on an f#, ending with a secondary cadence (g-d-f#). It then moves to the main cadence on the subdominant (A), a dramatic pause right in the middle of the sentence before the cry, *all the wicked of the earth*, with a double ornament on the single syllable כֹּל, *all*. It is remarkable to see the end of the sentence so separated from its beginning.

There is some irony in coming back to Isaiah. The question *who believes what we have heard* might now be about the strangeness of the music.

ISAIAH 53

Verse 1 begins on the f. Only 198 verses (0.8%) begin on the f. It seems to add some mystery to the text, besides suggesting that the verse is connected to the prior one. Yet the non-melismatic pulse of this verse suggests a new section of the song:

The music begins with a 14 beat low recitation on the tonic. This contrasts with what will follow in verses 3 and 4.

I have used *set aside* since the stem is חדל rather than *rejected* where the stem would be זנח. The music approaches the high recitation note but does not stay for long.

The word *contagion*, in Hebrew (נגע) as in English, derived from touch, is also in Psalm 91, a psalm of promise and consolation.

PSALM 91

The cost to the servant is severe.

That word *chastening* is in the psalm of the lectionary for Easter day in all years.

Forced (פגע) is an unexpected word. I have used it to reflect its usage in Ruth 2 and the importance of being in a safe place, safe for Ruth from Naomi's point of view, clearly vulnerable and unsafe for the servant in this passage.

RUTH 2

Choosing a gloss is a serious and creative set of decisions. *Force, might, strength*, and so on are compromised in their tone when such synonyms are randomly chosen. One can sometimes excuse the requirement for literary effect. It was common practise in some cultures, to frown on repeated words, but repeated words and their patterns are foundational in Hebrew poetry and important in recognizing when distant texts reflect each other.

Force here may be as simple as an encounter, but note that two of its letters overlap with *touch*. In some cases, the force may have the sense of assault, a very negative encounter. *Force* will come up again in verse 12.

This song like all the servant songs in the book of consolation, chapters 40 to 55, are traditionally applied to explain the character and work of Jesus. It is reasonable to note that the songs would have made perfect sense to the person(s) who wrote them. While they certainly can be applied and apply to Jesus, they also apply to the oppressed in all generations.

ISAIAH 53

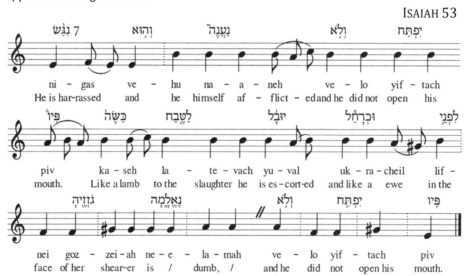

What does the composer of this music hear and intend when one reciting note is chosen in preference to another? This verse 7 has a 20-beat recitation on the fifth. Verse 8 like verse 5 has recitations on the sixth. The fifth is perhaps more stable harmonically, the sixth more in tension.

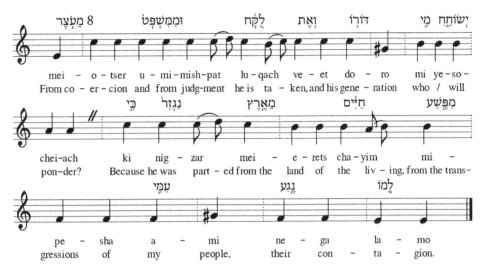

Again note the recurrence of the root for *touch* (contagion). Some Hebrew words require several glosses in translation. In the case of the very common word *strike* (נכה), usually used by translations here, to date I have not required a synonym. If we come back to Job, *touch* is exactly the word used. But is it *his* contagion, or the people's?

JOB 19

ISAIAH 53

He is generous with his death, the only thing that he has to give away. Yet in verse 10, he will see his seed, so in some sense there is more than survival through this generous gift of his death.

The Song in the Night

Note how *delight of Yahweh* frames verse 10.

68

This is not poetry like the poetry of the Psalms. The phrases are longer, the parallels more occasional, the recurrence patterns more varied though still present.

Who else is God's servant? It's a long answer, and I will leave you to work out the music for Abraham, Genesis 26.24; Moses, Numbers 12.7; Caleb, Numbers 14.24; David, 2 Samuel 3.18; Job, Job 1.8; Isaiah 22.20 (2 people mentioned), Israel, Isaiah 41.8, and specially Isaiah 42.19 with its hear/see imagery again; Jacob (=Israel) Isaiah 44.1; Nebuchadnezzar, Jeremiah 25.29; Zerubbabel, Haggai 2.23.These are the first instance of many in some cases.

Psalm 18 (below under Trust) contains an example of the confidence that is in David as the servant. Psalm 111 (below under Redeemed) shows that the human must not preclude itself in this same role. It is a characteristic of the servant that it learns obedience. Obedience is from the Latin *ob + audire* (to hear). How can we hear without training our ears to hear the music? So David is known as a musician (as noted above under Monarchy).

6. Restoration

Trust

Ultimately in the face of disaster, trust is called for.

This is another example where Kugel (1981 :116) says the pause contradicts the parallelism. Wickes (1881 :24) bases his positioning of accents on the parallelism. This is frequent but not always followed. In all cases that I look at, the passage is fine with the musical interpretation of the accents. In this case, the repetition of titles for Yahweh is very common in the Psalms. They are not always 'in parallel'. A good example is Psalm 18.3.

This passage is repeated in the prose books over two verses. And the words are varied.

The composer feels free to pile on additional devotions with a different pulse, no longer constrained by the shorter lines of the poetry genre.

Psalm 18:20-25 is an example of a circular structure: *turn*, *kept*, *not* with a focus of *before*, framed by *righteousness*, *purity* and *hands*, and it shows several parallelisms, (MacDonald 2014 :131). Verse 20 stands out as one that is lightly connected to the rest of the poem. The only recurrence for verse 20 is רחב (*broad*, *spacious*) also used in verse 37.

PSALM 18

Each verse in this section rises to the rest point on A. The repeated words of verses 21 and 25 are set to musical phrases of the same shape. Notice how each verse except the central verse 23 begins and ends on E. The uniqueness of verse 23 is confirmed by both the music and the recurrence pattern. The recitation on the rest note is less common than on the tonic, dominant or submediant.

Returned

To be restored, to have been restored, is implied in every section of the scriptural story. Psalm 1 begins with a statement of the one who is happy for having not wandered into a troubled path. It opens with alliteration on the sound of *sh*.

PSALM 1

In contrast, the psalm continues, such a one delights in the instruction of Yahweh. Again as a gloss I chose *instruction*, so that our legalistic framework will not be raised by the traditional *law*. Instruction is fearful enough for some, but it is personal and not an abstraction.

In these verses, the rise and fall of the diminished fifth will present little problem to singers of Bach.

In the grand analogy that is the Song of Solomon, there is a play on the *sh-l-m* sound in two verses, which, in a stretch, frames much of the poem. The first is the one with the *foxes*, (שׁועלים).

SONG 2

And the second, the one with the *Shulamite, she who has peace* (שׁולמית). The Shulamite is called to *return* (שׁוב). Return starts with the same *shu* sound.

The repeated *return* recalls the depth of this word, *turning* to Yahweh, the God of Israel.

LAMENTATIONS 5

Similar requests recur in the Psalms.

PSALM 80

Consoled

Turn is often translated as *repent*. Psalm 90 is a play on *turning* (verse 3). You *turn* (תָּשֵׁב *tashev*) a mortal to contrition, and you say *turn*, (שׁוּבוּ *shuvu*) children of humanity.

PSALM 90

Then in verses 8 and 9, there is a play on *face* (sometimes translated as *turn away*): our dissembling in the light of your *face* (פָּנֶיךָ *paneka*).

The Song in the Night

ki kol ya-mei-nu pa — nu ve-ev-ra — te-ka ki-li-nu sha — nei-nu ke-mo he-geh
For all our days face a — way from your / fu-ry. We con-sume our years as a / mut-ter.

For all our days *face away* (פָנוּ *panu*) from your fury. But here is the real turning, Yahweh's *turning*, known by Moses and the psalmist and completed such that God no longer needs to 'repent' but can *comfort*.

shu — vah ado-nai ad ma — tai ve — hi-na-cheim al a — va — dei-ka
Re — turn Yahweh, / how long? And be com — fort — ed over your ser-vants.

"So it will be that *the pleasure of the Lord our God* is upon us, astonishingly, a gift we need not turn away from, and equally, one in whom the Most High need not 'repent'" MacDonald (2013 :293). *Repent* is a gloss I have not used in my translations of the Hebrew (so far). To repent (rethink, reform, "change one's mind") is a far more complex and difficult process than simply to turn. Why make faith a psychological issue? Such a move keeps us second-guessing ourselves.

Console or consolation is not limited as in the commonplace phrase, consolation prize. In the New Testament, Simeon (Luke 2.25) is said to be waiting for the consolation of Israel. The root in Hebrew and in Greek has the legal sense of advocacy, hence the term for the 'Comforter' or 'Advocate' for the Holy Spirit, not a second class legal representative.

Isaiah 40 begins with the famous opening of Handel's Messiah.

ISAIAH 40

na — cha — mu na-cha — mu a — mi yo — mar e — lo-hei — kem
Com — fort, com-fort / / my people, says / / / your God.

dab — ru al leiv ye — ru-sha-lai — m ve — qir — u ei — lei — ah
Speak to the heart of Je — ru-sal-lem and / call to her for

ki mal — ah tse — va — ah ki nir — tsah a — vo — nah
full is her pressed ser — vice, for accepted is her in — iquity.

ki laq — chah mi — yad ado-nai kif — lai-yim be-kol cha-to — tei-ah
for she has re-ceived from the hand of Yah-weh / dou-ble in all / her sins. /

The word is not *pardoned*, but *accepted* (רצה). Perhaps it should have been *pardoned*, but it is not what is there.

Verse 3 is used in the New Testament in Matthew 3.3. The music may or may not support his parsing of the grammar of the text. The music can join or disjoin. But the accent on *calls* can be interpreted as a comma (as it is in the second part of the verse).

Implicit in the metaphors is the cost of sin and the repayment or redemption price that must be paid. The parable that is Psalm 49 plays on this problem.

PSALM 49

The price of acceptance is *a double,* an equal for sins, and who can afford it? But the cost, that is without price, is a gift that is offered.

ISAIAH 55

Redeemed

Cover-price (כפר) is the root of the word for the mercy-seat (כפרת, see Chapter 3 above) so the idea of payment is implicit in the building of the Sanctuary. Payment as acceptance for the one who brings the offering is said to be effected in the cult sacrifice, the life of the animal for the life of the one who brings the offering.

LEVITICUS 4

Yet, as Psalm 50 points out, God does not want the blood of bulls or goats.

PSALM 50

Redemption is not a bribe, though the word can be used in that sense as we saw in Samuel's defense of his behaviour as leader and judge. Redemption is celebrated by Psalm 110, the second of two oracles in the Psalms.

PSALM 110

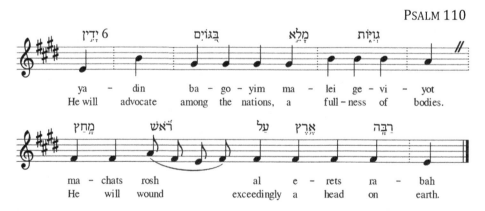

Psalm 110 is in turn celebrated by the acrostics, Psalms 111-112. Each of these miniatures is 10 verses, 8 bi-cola covering the first 16 letters and two tri-cola for the last 6 letters. The P-S-Q (פ צ ק) verse picks up the cost of redemption for the people. Tsade is a hard letter to use in English so in this case I have used an S.

PSALM 111

Purchase price, distinct from *cover price*, is from the word for *ransom*. The metaphor extends itself to the people in a state of captivity, unable to pay the cost of such ransom. Redemption like wrath, is directed to the desire of God to live with his people.

Isaiah 12, six short verses, identifies the purpose of anger. In it we are told to sing a psalm. Psalm 6, which we began with in Chapter 1, is suitable to the message.

PSALM 6

The whole story and purpose of God is in the Psalms, a very human collection of poems. Isaiah 12 quotes or alludes to Psalm 118, Exodus 15, and Psalm 105.

PSALM 118

Here's a lesson in underlay. Note in Isaiah 12, Exodus 15, and Psalm 118, the accent on *my*, (לִי). A translated libretto should reflect this emphasis.

PSALM 105

ISAIAH 12

Praise

The fifth book of the Psalms is full of praise. The Halleluiahs begin even at the end of Book 4. At some point one has to get serious about why the Bible is important and how to read it without getting sidetracked by distractions. For there is no doubt there are many distractions.

There is first a *time-dependent* distraction. We have some notion of time in the 21st century. We do not live in the time in which these works were written, if indeed time is ultimately so important. If we have learned the limits of time from Einstein, then we should not be surprised at the presence of all time in a founding moment like the Exodus or Passover, or indeed of the presence of the unknown, creating, instructing, and redeeming in our own personal lives, even in their institutional patterns filled with local customs.

There is also a *political* distraction. Certainly this is true of Psalm 135 which we must somehow set in its place. If we have no table, it is hard to set it. If our table is lopsided, the settings will fall off. If we have no floor, the table will disappear when we place something on it in the gravity of the moment.

PSALM 135

Is this poem purely nationalistic and self-serving? But more importantly, what precedes this psalm? It is more than half way through Book 5 of the Psalter. Book 3 has detailed the failure of the monarchy of Israel and Judah. Book 4 has detailed renewal from the disaster of the monarchy. *Renewal* is a significant frame for the book. Book 4 is framed by *Moses* and two prayers: 90, of Moses, and 102, a prayer of the disabled.

PSALM 90

Renewal then is through prayer and the instruction (Torah) of Yahweh, the God of Israel. (And here is a *religious* distraction: Torah is not rule-bound though it is read that way by millions.) Torah defines Israel. Israel so defined is *an example to the rest of the world* of what not to do in your own defense. (*Political and religious* distractions.)

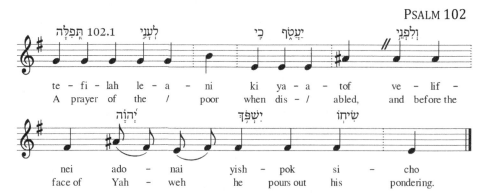

So when, in this Psalm 135, we read that Israel is beloved, *a treasure trove to Yahweh*, and then hear a little more, from Job.

Then we ask, does Yahweh, the God of Israel, *ache* for Israel? Israel whom he rescued and who wandered for 40 years, and who sinned in the land, and whom he exiled and then restored. Relationships are fractured in Jerusalem like nowhere else in the world. How long will it hold together using walls and razor wire?

Does the same God *ache* for all creation? Wait, you say, Is God not completely without feelings by definition? This is a serious question about theory. We could use a lot of big words like omniscient, impassive, omnipresent, immortal, invisible. But big words don't make for a good story, a good drama, or good music. Nor do they engage anyone apart from an explaining intellectual with a different need from most people.

That which is called Yahweh, God, in the Hebrew texts that we consider in this book, or Allah, the Merciful in the Quran, or the God of Jesus in the New Testament, according to what we have seen and heard in these musical examples, that Other is not without feeling or interest in the created order. Hidden, perhaps, as gravity waves, only recently dimly heard, but not without feeling. Even the scientist said, 'Gravity does not like to be disturbed'. What a strange statement, as if gravity had feelings! Bigness too is not necessarily indifferent. Nor is it descriptive. All those powerful particles in the universe are very small. So unlike the scaling factors of light years or neutrinos, the God of the Psalms is not indifferent. Nor am I, nor are you. Did we do all this ourselves?

Psalm 135 follows the 15 Psalms of Ascent. These are thought to have been sung as a sequence, one on each of the temple steps. Psalm 135 and Psalm 136 celebrate the arrival in the courts of Yahweh. (These 2 psalms are practically identical in length and share a host of keywords, 20 of them in the same sequence).

The first verses show the arrival in the courts and reflect some of the complexity of the musical accents that we saw in the Decalogue (disproving the thesis that there are two conflicting sets of signs in the Decalogue, but that's *academic* distraction.)

PSALM 135

All that delighted Yahweh, he did. Yahweh has a lot to answer for. When will we demand the answer and how will we respond to the requirement to fix the mess we have made with God's creation (the mist) and redemption (the slaying of the firstborn) and in all time, the treasury of spirit. What an immense cost. What a God of terror and fear. Who would want to be his *treasure trove*? What sort of spirit are we from?

Is this political? In the sense of justice, most certainly. We must get on with the salvaging of refugees, stop the violence towards others, find a containment for radicalization. It's up to us because God is depending on us.

There is no magical *Deus ex Machina*. There is our responsibility with the blessing of the Invisible and I should add the Unspeakable. Words are stopped by the tension between description and conviction, or by the impassiveness of scholarship and the demands of faithfulness. Knowledge comes through juxtaposition rather than solely by explanation. Hearing the mystery, the same that encountered Moses, with faithfulness likewise for us encounters an inexplicable response. Pondering the brief three-word phrase of Habakkuk may suffice: *but-the-righteous-one in-his-faithfulness will-live.*

If we are those who stand singing in the courts of Yahweh, there can be no inflated triumphalism. We are a charade (Meshek) living in blackness (Qeidar). Charade and blackness are usually transliterated as place names.

But there is help, as this traditional Psalm at funerals notes.

Also there is responsibility for the pomegranate in razor wire that is the partnered Jerusalem.

There is enough contempt to go around.

The Song in the Night

cha - nei - nu ado - nai cha - nei nu   ki rav   sa - va - nu   vuz
Be gracious to us Yahweh be gracious to us. for ex-ceed - ingly we are sated with con - tempt.

Our help enables escape.

PSALM 124

naf - shei - nu ke - tsi - por nim - le - tah   mi - pach yoq -
Our be - ing as a bird / es - caped from snare of

shim ha - pach nish - bar va - a - nach - nu nim - lat - nu
trappers. The snare is bro - ken and we ourselves have es - caped.

Good receives good.

PSALM 125

hei - ti - vah   ado - nai la - to - vim   ve -
Do good /   Yah - weh to the good, and

li - sha - rim   be - li - bo - tam
to the up - right in their hearts.

There are tears in the night but joy in the morning.

PSALM 126

ha - zor - im be - dim - ah   be - ri - nah yiq - tso - ru
/ Those sow - ing in tears with a shout of joy will har - vest.

There is joy in children. (And payment.)

PSALM 127

hi - neih na - cha - lat adonai ba - nim   sa - kar pe - ri ha - baten
Here! children are an in - her - i - tance of Yahweh, the fruit of the bel-ly a wage.

PSALM 128

ur – eih va – nim le – va – nei – ka sha – lom al yis – ra – eil
And you will see your children's / chil-dren, and peace up-on Isra-el.

And there is plenty of trouble.

PSALM 129

ra – bat tse – ra – ru – ni min – u – rai gam lo yak – lu li
Ex–ceed-ingly they trou-bled me from my youth, al – though they have not over – powered me.

Watch and wait.

PSALM 130

naf – shi la – do – nai mi – shom –
My being for my Lord, more than those

rim la – bo – qer shom – rim la – bo – qer
watching for the morning, those watching for the morn – ing.

There are wonders beyond us. Dependency and growth are possible.

PSALM 131

shir ha – ma – a lot le–da – vid ado – nai lo ga – vah li–bi ve–lo ra – mu ei – nai ve–
A song of the ascents, of Da – vid. Yah – weh / not haughty is my heart nor ex – alted my eyes, nor

lo hi – lak – ti big – do – lot uv – nif – la – ot mi – me – ni
do I walk in / great things / or in wonders be – yond me.

There is a rest that belongs to Yahweh.

The Song in the Night

PSALM 132

qu – mah ado-nai lim-nu-cha – te-ka a – tah va-a – ron u – ze – ka
A – rise Yahweh in-to your rest, you and the / ark of your strength. /

It is good to live in unity with your kin.

PSALM 133

shir ha-ma-a – lot le – da – vid hi – neih mah tov u – mah na –
A song of the ascents, of Da vid. / Here! How fine and how /

im she – vet a – chim gam ya – chad
pleasant it is for kin to sit as one.

Who is it makes heaven and earth?

PSALM 134

ye – va – rek – ka ado – nai mi – tsi – yon o – seih sha –
Yah – weh will bless you / out of Zion, who makes /

mai – yim va – a – rets
hea – ven and earth.

Such trust, waiting, and watching are not a recipe for passivity. Our action, our part will be called out of us.

The great acrostic, Psalm 119, a celebration of the psalm just preceding it, begins with this statement of joy and happiness.

PSALM 119

ash – rei te – mi – mei da – rek ha – hol – kim be – to – rat ado – nai
All joy for the com – plete of the way. / who walk in the in – struction of Yahweh.

PSALM 112

tov ish cho – nein u – mal – veh ye – kol –
This is a good person, gra-cious and lending. Yea, he will

In effect, the Psalms are saying, terrible it may be, but it is a God who cares (as if

keil de – va – rav be – mish – pat
rein in his words with / judgment.

God is like the good person of Psalm 112) for the dispossessed.

Psalm 146.6-9 encapsulates the character of Yahweh. This summary goes beyond culture, social structure, or national or personal self-interest. Such a God, defined in the text as the one who makes heaven and earth, the sea and all that is in it, undermines both the idea and the motivations of mere survival of the fittest. The accents in the first verses of the last five psalms tie all these psalms together as a unit.

PSALM 146

In all the above, the *who* is a relative and not an interrogative pronoun. Is it true that we naturally relegate God to the past or the future? Here, God is in the present.

It is true that this character of caring is also present in the body of the people. It is encouraging that the street people are being fed, refugees are being processed and the endangered species are being studied and protected. Obviously there is great difficulty, and the source of power and strength for us to do what is right is not obvious. We could easily retreat, easily retrench, turn back to our own self-protection (and sometimes this is needed).

The wholeness of marmalade requires bitter orange full of the spirit of its inedible seed. In the fullness of time, after a little boiling following the application of heat, there is jelled sweetness in the outcome.

PSALM 150

Everyone is called to praise:

Psalm 117, a mere two verses, is the shortest chapter in the Bible. Here are its two verses as introduction to the invitation to praise for all peoples and all tribes and all clans.

Notice that there is a rest for *nations*, but there is no rest in verse 2. This Psalm can be rendered with a regular 7 pulse phrase. The two verses are so short, you can sing them three times in just over a minute. Here is a da capo arrangement with the opening and closing in the Lydian mode, and the middle two verses in the default psalms mode but with a sharpened sixth. And let children play the wooden blocks with gusto taking care not to pinch their fingers on the down beat.

7. Haïk-Vantoura's system

The parts of the text

In our typical Latin-based texts, we have 26 letters, words separated by spaces, and punctuation. The letters are either vowels or consonants, a single letter (like Y or W) occasionally acting as either. Latin based punctuation is accomplished through fewer than a dozen marks. In the Hebrew Scriptures, there are 22 consonants, a dozen or so vowels, and the *te'amim*, a set of about two dozen marks or *accents*, considered for the last 1000 years as *punctuation*. Mitchell (2012) dubs them "punctuation on steroids".[16]

Letter	Rough pronunciation		Letter	Rough pronunciation
א Alef	guttural or nothing		ל Lamed	l
ב Bet	b or v		מ ם Mem	m
ג Gimel	g (hard)		נ ן Nun	m
ד Daleth	d or th		ס Samech	s
ה Heh	h		ע Ayin	guttural deeper than *alef*
ו Vav	ꞷ va ꞷ oo ꞷ ve ꞷ vo ꞷ vi ꞷ veh ꞷ va ꞷ or nothing		פ ף Peh	p or f
ז Zayin	z		צ ץ Tsade	ts
ח Chet	ch		ק Qof	q
ט Tet	t		ר Resh	r
י Yod	y		שׁ Shin	sh
כ ך Kaf	k		שׂ Sin	s
			ת Taf	t

The table above lists the letters and vowels (all shown under the letter vav). Separate from these are the accents. Both vowels and accents are under and over the letters of

the text, like this letter bet with an 'a' under it, בַ pronounced *ba or va*. The accents,

also called marks of taste,[17] like this mark, בֱ, can be considered as disjunctive or conjunctive signs like punctuation, but they are of sufficient complexity taken together, to be hand signals, signs indicating the movements of a conductor of music. They consist of two overlapping sets of signs, one for the Psalms, Proverbs, and the speeches of Job, and one for all the rest of the Hebrew Bible.

---

[16] As noted in Chapter 1 above, if one is thinking they are syllabic stress first and word-separation second, then one does not have to think of them as punctuation.

[17] The word טעם *ta'am*, taste, from which the name of the accents is derived, can also mean a slight madness. Both these meanings are evident in the alphabetic acrostic poem, Psalm 34, verses 1 and 9 in the Hebrew numbering. In verse 1, David feigns his madness so he can escape from Abimelech, and in the first word of verse 9 (*tet* being the ninth letter of the alef-bet) the poet uses the same word to mean *taste*. Note that Wickes (1881 :4) in what I must assume is a bias towards meaning, defines te'amim as *meanings*. Wickes as a result wants to correct the signs based on *meaning*. But if meaning is subordinate to music, not superior to it, such corrections will be retrograde.

Figure 12 The deciphering key

The notes of the poetry scale are named as follows (left to right):

galgal, silluq, merkha, tifha, atnah, munah, mahpakh.
wheel, end, extension, palm, resting, placed, returned.

The prose notes that are not in the poetry scale are darga (*step,* low c) and tevir (*broken,* low d instead of galgal).

The first thing to note about these accents is that there are exactly eight signs *below* the letters for the prose and seven for the poetry. The first two of the prose and the first of the poetry are different. Otherwise the remaining 6 signs are identical.

The second thing to notice takes some reading. The signs below the letters are never absent. They occur on every verse. The signs above *may be absent* for whole sections of text. There are 3,188 verses completely without any supra-linear signs.

The signs below must therefore be more important than the signs above. What a musician might notice is that the signs below could be applied to a musical scale, the full octave for the prose, and a seven-note scale for the poetry.[18]

The remaining signs, with some duplication of those used below the letters, all occur above the letters. There are eleven in use for the prose and eight for the poetry. The overlap between the sets is quite comprehensible to a musician. It is not difficult to learn to sight-read the music, much as a musician can sight-read tonic sol-fa.

The deciphering key

The French organist and composer, Suzanne Haïk-Vantoura, in the last half of the 20th century, following much experimentation, inferred that the signs below the letters for the prose books correspond exactly to a tonic sol-fa scale with a raised fifth: c d e f, g# A B C. Her default setting for the poetry scale is: d# e f# g A B C.

In the winter of 2014, I wrote a computer program with rules based on her work, to convert the Hebrew text into Music XML. In contrast to the lexical problem where the derivation of a stem may lead to more than one possible result, or to the grammatical problem without vowels, that the same letters can be read in contradictory ways, the music conversion is well defined. When a set of rules is applied, it is unambiguous, indicating that these Scriptures are a programmed art-form from ancient minds.

All these pitches are relative to the tonic (e = doh in moveable doh solfege), the third note of the prose scale and the second note of the poetry scale.[19] The tonic is signified

---

[18] Mitchell (2015) points out that a sign known from the Aleppo Codex has been dropped from the poetry: "Sometimes this circular galgal symbol would seem to suit a high note, as in Psalm 122.4, where it sings the ascent of the tribes, and sometimes a low note, as at the bowing-down in Psalm 138.2." I have not considered this additional sign in my analysis. Whether high or low, I have noted that high and low may be ironic word-painting, the opposite of what one might expect.

by the *silluq*, under the letter. This sign occurs at the end of every verse. The vast majority of verses also come to a point of rest on the A subdominant. The sign, ^ the *atnah*, is the primary disjunctive mark in all such verses.

Haïk-Vantoura interpreted the set of signs that occur above the letters as ornaments relative to the current pitch. The current pitch is determined by default as the tonic until a sign is encountered that changes it. The current pitch remains the reciting note until a new sign is encountered below the letters. The ornaments return to the current pitch either on the current syllable or on the next syllable. The determination is made based on placement of the sign and whether the pitch changes on the next syllable. It sometimes seems to be subjective.

Here are the ornaments for the prose books as they would be interpreted on a musical staff when the current pitch is A.

Figure 13 Ornaments for the 21 books

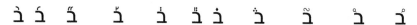

And here are the ornaments for the poetry books again based on the current pitch as A.

Figure 14 Ornaments for the 3 books

The names for the poetry books (left to right) are:

qadma (pre) or pashta (post), geresh, revia, illuy, one note each; pazer, ole, zarqa (tsinnor), shalshelet, are each a melisma.

These names have interpretations: *stretcher, expulsion, crouching, elevated, dispersing, ascending* and *descending, tube, chain.* Note the ole followed by merkha is called ole-veyored, and is an important secondary cadence in the 3 books. The sequence of supra-lineal signs, geresh-revia (revia-mugrash) is common in the 3 books (following the atnah, or by itself if there is no atnah).

There are six ornaments that are different in the 21 books, the double geresh (or tarsin בֿ), zaqef qatan (upright small בֿ), zaqef gadol (upright big בֿ), segol (bunch of grapes בֿ), and the two horns, qarne farah (both horns together), telisha (detached בֿ) qetanah/gedolah (בֿ). You will understand why I do not use these names. And they all have alternative names and multiple different spellings in differing Hebrew traditions or in different books and articles. There is a little more about them in Appendix 3.

---

[19] The choice of E is arbitrary and may be adjusted to a lower pitch if singers or instruments require it.

In all the many examples developed by Haïk-Vantoura, she says she has applied these notes *without exception* to decipher the music from the Hebrew text.[20] She recommends using the Max HaLevi Letteris edition (1896). Mitchell (2013)[21] points out that her bias is not justified in that she likely never saw the more reliable Aleppo Codex. All the music in this volume has been derived from the Hebrew text of the Westminster Leningrad codex (www.tanach.us/Tanach.xml) and the rules have been applied by the program. Note that if new rules come to light or a new source of data is available, applying the programming to the new data or adjusting it to new rules is a straightforward task.

Modes

The 3 books, 7 note scale

Chromatic hypodorian Lydian (limited major)   Lydian with minor 6th   Hypodorian
                                                                            pronounced chromatic

The 21 books, 8 note scale

Chromatic dorian   Hypodorian -   Lydian   Chromatic Phrygian
                   diatonic minor   with augmented 4th

Figure 15 Modes as used by Haïk-Vantoura

Determining the mode (Haïk-Vantoura 1991 :349) of a particular section of the text is a subjective exercise. It may be that some note patterns are unacceptable in some modes. This is an uncertain decision, since instrument and voice can each be tuned to any of these modes. Equally, it may be that some sections even if sung together were sung in two differing modes. If different tuning is required, then two instruments may be prepared.

Singing

Haïk-Vantoura suggests two differing approaches to the singing. For the prose, she assumes an imprecise word based rhythm. It does not require 'precision, seeing that it is framed on verbal discourse' (1976 :54). In equally vague terms, she insists on a syllabic pulse after the manner of plainchant for the poetry. In practice, there is little to differentiate these. And the performances indicate that syllables are important in a word-based free rhythm as words are important in a syllable-based rhythm. One should not throw syllables away or garble them in any case. That is, in all texts, syllables 'gather themselves together equally' in ones, twos, threes, fours, fives, and so on, each group creating a 'beat' in the musical line subdivided into syllables of equal duration with little if any additional word stress. Ornaments will naturally extend a syllable's length and will interpret the words. This is true whether one is thinking of the 'words' or of their syllables. In modern notation, recitation may be

---

[20] Haïk-Vantoura is subjective at some points especially in mode 4, rejecting the A# where it suits her taste. Nonetheless, her consistency is very high if not as rigid as a computer program will be. Her rules are absolute compared with those of Wickes.
[21] Mitchell (2013). In his later work (2015) he notes that Letteris is the most muddled of the 20th century editions.

spelled out in 'notes' but note values are not to be slavishly interpreted. Having noted this, it is possible that some psalms were sung rhythmically. Where this may be the case for Hebrew, an equivalent rhythm in translation may be searched for. Haïk-Vantoura writes that there is to be a constant duration for a syllable in the poetry. It is clear from attempted musical reconstructions of performance today that this claim is an approximation.

Pulse

In my transcriptions, a dashed bar line immediately precedes a change in reciting note. The direction of the vocal line and its pulse is thus signaled by the bar-line (in some images I have manually broken these bars up to enable music in the boundaries of a smaller book). The underlay of the translation should be done with consideration for this musical impulse.

The subdominant A is signaled by the sign called atnah, or place of rest. In mode 4, the A is sharpened and acts against any suggestion of rest or repose. Note also that some verses have no rest point and may sometimes be chanted as a single phrase. Some verses have multiple phrases, but never more than one primary rest point. The rest point is marked with a caesura indicating the appropriateness of a pause – even in the middle of a sentence, as one would pause in plainsong to allow consideration of the words.

The Hebrew pulse and accents may suggest other possible performance ideas or word underlay to the choir director. Such performance ideas are encouraged. Since many of the psalms are 'for the choir director', choir directors may of course use their discretion in suggesting alternatives with respect to mode, rhythm or pitch or even the interpretation of ornaments.

Awkward intervals

Yes, there are some awkward intervals but they can be learned and often are surprising annotations on the text. Psalm 4 provides a good example. The emphasis on the ornaments and the rising augmented fifth in verse 7 colour the extreme rudeness and provocation in the words. The music confirms the quotation marks noted in some translations.

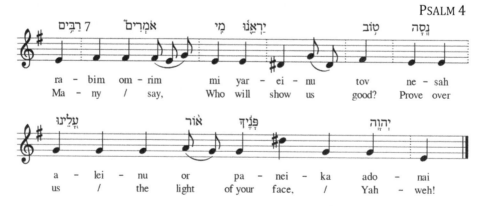

The next rising perfect fifth in verse 8 contrasts provocation with the joy in the gift.

Word painting

The music is not there for its own sake, but for the words. For every text, the music provides what one could call an intense phrasing, demanding from singer and hearer alike an intention that goes behind the habitual and becomes clothing indeed.

Psalm 32 provides a good example. Note the bucking horse and mule (verse 9). Note also the word, curbed, on the atnah or rest point in the verse. This word is a hapax, occurring only here in the Hebrew Bible.

PSALM 32

Words on the atnah in the other verses are: *iniquity*, *bones worn out*, *changed*, *Yahweh*, *many waters*, *security*, *walk*, *Yahweh*, and *righteous ones*. There is a progression in this psalm from trouble to release including the reference to the judgment of many waters and the need for a secure guided walk for the poet and singer.

Arrangements

It will be abundantly clear that there is enough possible arranging of this music for millennia. With respect to the simple underlay, I have in the examples taken one of several possible approaches:

- Verse in Hebrew with translated words not set as libretto. This is the least satisfactory from a translation point of view, but it is good to sing in Hebrew.
- Translated words set with symbols and bar lines to indicate suggested underlay. This is possible, as in books of plainsong or chant, but it is limited. It has the advantage of avoiding a wooden pulse that may be implied with a libretto in the score itself.
- Translation set as a libretto. To do this, download the XML file from the Web and use a music program. This is easy to read but a little more time-consuming for the arranger. It also allows a more thorough criticism of the translation and its pulse compared to the Hebrew.

Where I have a translated libretto, I use the symbol / to indicate that the note is not needed and has therefore a zero time value. If I have omitted the / after an ornament, the slurred syllable may include the return to the reciting note. If there are multiple syllables on a slurred ornament, slur then append the additional syllable to imitate the style of the Hebrew. If I omit the / where you would expect one, consider lengthening the prior syllable or including it in the melisma. If the translated libretto has multiple syllables for a single note, then subdivide all the syllables and gather them equally into the current note.

If you are designing an underlay, try to preserve with the least compromise the line and stress of the Hebrew. So wherever possible, without distorting the translated word order beyond recognition, you can try to place ornaments on an equivalent syllable and slur as in the Hebrew and let the change in reciting note reflect a similar word and stress as in the Hebrew. It is evident that sometimes the translated gloss and pulse match the Hebrew word for word, but equally, sometimes there must be compromises made when trying to match words in the musical line. Rework the translated underlay as required. Note that there are particular difficulties with maintaining Hebrew letter order in translation of an acrostic where the poet is at play, if sometimes reluctantly.

A transcription from signs to a musical score requires much more than notes. Even with the notes, how do we know that ornamentation was fixed as Haïk-Vantoura has suggested? Yet her ornaments work (to a degree). Then there are questions of mode and rhythm, of multi-voice possibilities, responsive psalms, harmony, and accompaniment.

Haïk-Vantoura suggests several modes. Are there clues in the inscriptions (of the psalms that have them) that would allow us to associate a mode with a psalm? Are there clues in the music? Certain patterns are the same in more than one mode. Some patterns may be harder to sing in one mode rather than another.

All sorts of instruments may be used. Composers and arrangers are encouraged to find the appropriate registers. In some psalms like Psalms 2 and 150, percussion seems invited. In the absence of tympani, hand-clapping or striking a hard surface with the palm may produce the desired effect. All the psalms work very well unaccompanied. It is also feasible to add vocal parts to the implied harmonies. Haïk-Vantoura's Psalm 98 is a very good example.

To reflect the separation of voices in the text itself and occasionally also highlight rhetorical structure, verses or parts of verses may be assigned to differing voices: one or two cantors, and up to 9 chorus combinations, Men, Women, Tutti and each divided or not between Cantoris and Decani. Mitchell (2015), chapters 9 and 10, has excellent background on instruments and chorus parts.

Translation

In my translations, I have, through the use of software algorithms constantly checking my work, deliberately chosen different glosses to correspond to different Hebrew words. So, for example, if there are 7 synonyms for *fear* in the Hebrew, so there are 7 different words in the translation for these words. Similarly, a word used only once requires a gloss in the translation that is used only once. At the same time, some words require differing glosses in differing contexts. For example, the word, *nefesh*, traditionally translated *soul*, has as its primary gloss that part of the body between chin and shoulders, the *throat*. I never use *soul* because Hebrew is too concrete to allow the disembodied to rule. But sometimes I use *being*, or *self*, or even just a personal pronoun. So sometimes a single word in Hebrew will be rendered in the host language by several differing words or combinations of words.

The Name

In many translations, the Name, יהוה, the four letters yod, heh, vav, heh, is rendered as the LORD. Such a rendering fails both grammatically and theologically: theologically because the Name is intimate and personal, grammatically, because the Name must behave as a proper name, not as title or rank. Debate is extensive over how the Name was pronounced or when it stopped being said as a name. In my earlier work I left the Name in Hebrew letters. In the music, in Hebrew, I substitute the perpetual qere (= to be read as). You can always distinguish the qere from a true instance of *Adonai*, because the qere is given only two syllables in the music transcription, and *Adonai* is always three. For the music I have used the mid-20th century rendering *Yahweh*. This may be sung as two or three syllables as needed. There is a suggestion from the stresses in the music that it was three syllables with the stress on the third. There are no consonants in the name. Sing it as Ee-aa-oo-eh with the oo bordering on an O. It is a good singing exercise. Mitchell (2015 Appendix I) has a good argument for the traditional Yehovah.

Invocations, selah and other words

The invocations or inscriptions of the Psalms and occasionally in the Prophets, are an integral part of the music, as are the interjections like *Selah* or *higgaion* whose meaning is uncertain. These have remained in the music as given. Use the moments creatively. The inscriptions in the Psalms are each unique and beautiful. Contrary to Wickes (1881 :35), there is nothing lacking in their accentuation.

The 21 Books and the 3 Books

The 24 Books are

- Torah: Genesis, Exodus, Leviticus, Numbers, Deuteronomy,
- The Former Prophets: Joshua, Judges, Samuel, Kings,
- The Latter Prophets: Isaiah, Jeremiah, Ezekiel, The Twelve (Hosea, Joel, Amos, Obadiah, Jonah, Micah, Nahum, Habakkuk, Zephaniah, Haggai, Zechariah, Malachi),
- The Books of Truth: Psalms, Proverbs, Job,
- The Five Scrolls: Song, Ruth, Lamentations, Qohelet, Esther
- The Remaining: Daniel, Ezra-Nehemiah, Chronicles.

The poetic accents are used only in the Books of Truth (though there are poetic-like sections of other books). Within these, the narrative sections of Job use the prose accents even to the point of switching from one set to another in a single chapter. All the narrator's introductions use the prose accents, but the speeches use the poetic accents. One might not notice, but occasionally there is one that stands out. Imagine the narrator changing instruments for the short introduction to a speech during the performance. The narrator's single verse introductions also vary in their start note. This clearly pairs each of Job's speeches with the speech that follows it.

History

The more serious question of the history of the signs is raised in Mitchell (2012 :11) and more thoroughly in his later work (2015).[22] How did the Masoretic system of the *te'amim* come into being? There is no history of this fully formed symbol system. His summary is very helpful:

1. Cantillation marks per se are found in 2nd millennium BCE in Sumerian literature. They are found on biblical texts in the Dead Sea Scrolls[23] and in the Babylonian and Palestinian accent systems, and are referred to in the Talmud.
2. However, the Masoretic system stands apart from its predecessors in its sudden appearance as a highly perfected system.
3. By the testimony of Mosheh Ben Asher himself, the Masoretes received the *te'amim* from the second-century BCE Elders of Bathyra. This conforms to the Masoretic credo of not innovating but preserving.
4. The Masoretes' rabbanite contemporaries, Natronai b. Hilai and Sa'adia, objected to the Masoretes' work not because the *te'amim* were a novelty, but because they thought them ancient but sealed.
5. The similarity of the Masoretic *te'amim* to the symbols of a third-century BCE text of Euripides shows that they are indeed musical symbols of pre-Christian times. For the Masoretes to have invented them would be as anachronistic as for us annotate a Bible in runes.

Mitchell's article also contains the example of *Tonus Peregrinus*, a known melody used in several traditions. Haïk-Vantoura never mentions this tune, yet her deciphering key applied to Psalm 114, demonstrates a tune that is very close to *Tonus Peregrinus*. Mitchell (2015 :146) concludes: *It follows that the Tonus Peregrinus is our best*

---

[22] I am encouraged that he cites an authority who found Aharon ben Mosheh's own commentary, *Diqduqe ha te'amim* (Fine points of the te'amim) 'for the most part incomprehensible'.

[23] The presence in very early Talmud is footnoted in place: "A discussion, attributed to the 1st-2nd century tanna Akiva, tells how the ta'amey-torah must be indicated with the right hand (B. Meg. 3a)".

remaining fragment of Temple Psalmody. Heller (2006 :105) points out this same melody as a traditional chant for Psalm 114 from Lithuania to Yemen.

At a minimum the signs go back to the 8th century CE where they appear fully formed in the Aleppo Codex of the Hebrew Bible. Mitchell's extended argument (2015 :133) suggests that the signs are much older. DeHoop (2013 :20) writes that there is evidence that the reading tradition reflected by the accents dates back to the beginning of the common era.

Christopher Smart, among my favorite poets has a note on the ACCENTS,[24]

> *For the ACCENTS are the invention of the Moabites, who learning the GREEK tongue marked the words after their own vicious pronuntiation.*
> *For the GAULS (the now-French and original Moabites) after they were subdued by Cœsar became such Grecians at Rome.*
> *For the Gaullic manuscripts fell into the hands of the inventors of printing.*
> *For all the inventions of man, which are good, are the communications of Almighty God.*

Unfortunately, I suspect that by *ACCENTS* he meant the vowels rather than the te'amim.

On a more serious note, Revell writes: "In a number of Biblical texts from Qumran, spaces are used to mark divisions in the text which correspond either to verse divisions, or to the divisions within the verses which are marked by the major disjunctive accents in the Hebrew Bible. Several Psalms texts are written in hemistichs, and thus show divisions corresponding not only to atnah and ole-weyored, the accents which mark the main verse divisions, but also to rebia and sinrior, which mark less important divisions. In 1Q5, 4 the text of Deut. 32 was written regularly with four hemistichs to a line, separated by spaces, which marked both main and lesser verse divisions (and so correspond to zaqef Deut. xxxii, 21, 22)" (1971 :214).

DEUTERONOMY 32

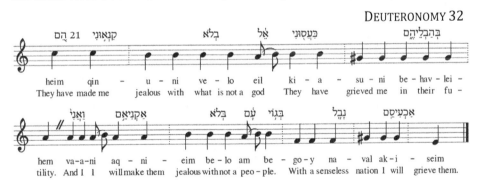

---

[24] Jubilate Agno, lines B398-401 cited in Tomalin (2009: 776) where he writes: 'In the standard critical editions of *Jubilate Agno*, these lines are explained by means of an association with Caesar's reference to the writing practices of the "Druides" in his *De Bello Gallico* (vi, 14).' Though we are considering reading and writing, the more interesting note in this section of Caesar's Wars, is Caesar's comment that writing leads to a relaxation of 'their diligence in learning thoroughly, and their employment of memory'. Writing may lead there, but if the Druides had been learning with musical accents, their memory would have been enhanced.

Revell further notes (1971 :222) that even the text of the earliest Greek Septuagint text shows patterns of separation according to the Hebrew accents: "Rylands Greek Pap. 458, then, already highly valued as the oldest known Septuagint text, is seen to have even greater significance. For the Septuagint, it provides, in combination with the other Greek texts discussed here, definite evidence that this version was used for formal lections in the Synagogue. For the Hebrew Bible, it shows clearly that the basis of the system of cantillation represented by the later accents was already firmly established in the second century B.C., and was so much a part of the formal reading of the Tora, that it was also used for the Septuagint."

The simplest summary

Imagine a very complex puzzle, all sorts of signs that are foreign and that read backwards to your usual thought. Vowels, aids to reading, that are consonants while the rest aren't visible. And then there are vowels there but they feel unreadable and unpronounceable. And then a third set of signs, call them accents, a lot of them, more than 20, that are traditionally interpreted as either complex chanted melismas or some kind of 'punctuation on steroids'. There are many explanations of them but only one that I have seen that makes these accents transparent.

Haïk-Vantoura inferred this transparent deciphering key in the period from 1940-1960.

"Born in Paris, France in 1912, she entered the Conservatoire National Superieur de Musique in Paris in 1931, and was awarded First Prize in Harmony (1934), First Prize in Fugue (1938), and Honorable Mention in Composition (1939). She became the student of the great organist and composer Marcel Dupré from 1941 to 1946, then devoted herself to music composition and teaching.

World War II interrupted her studies, and she fled with her family to southern France. While in hiding from the Nazis, then-Mlle. Vantoura first approached a problem that had intrigued her since childhood: the original meaning of the te'amim. By her account, she had learned in a French encyclopedia of music that these signs were ancient, musical and of unknown meaning. Given the lack of correlation between the melodies of the synagogue communities and the physical features of the notation itself, this appraisal was both plausible and objective, and it became the starting point in Mlle. Vantoura's research.

Finally, her old teacher Marcel Dupré and others urged her to complete her work. After her 'retirement' in 1970, she devoted herself to the task and (by her own testimony) was overwhelmed at times by the sheer scale of it. It took her four years to complete her decipherment, and another two years to prepare the first edition of her

French book La musique de la Bible révélée (Robert Dumas, 1976) and the Harmonia Mundi LP of the same name (also in 1976). The second edition of her French book (Dessain et Tolra, 1978) won the Prix Bernier of the Institute des Beaux Arts de France, at that time its highest award." (From Wheeler)

I feel very privileged to have been introduced to this brilliant set of inferences that opens up the Scripture like no other tool I can imagine. Music is at the heart of the Word of God. God is a musician. So we are instructed by singing and hearing as well as by sight and visual pattern.

The location for all the music

Haïk-Vantoura's insight is a key that can be applied to the entire text by a computer program. I have produced for the public the entire contents of the Leningrad codex[25] as a music score. It is an estimated 6000 pages of music, all online. The entry point for the music is this page. http://meafar.blogspot.ca/p/music.html. The music is in both portable document format (PDF) and music XML, an extended markup language that allowed me to translate the Hebrew text directly into musical notation along with all the original Hebrew and a transcription into Latin letters. It is also part of my continuing work to extend my translations to all 304,000 words of the Hebrew Bible.[26]

Once you begin to hear the music of these accents, there is no need for much further explanation of what the accents mean. An expressive musician can tell the story by singing the song. And what possibilities there are for performance. The music gives a dramatic new feel to familiar stories, instruction, and poetry from the Old Testament. It is quite feasible to perform a bilingual lesson with one singer singing the Hebrew and then another or the same interpreting by singing the same line in translation. Use as many different performers for individual characters as the scene requires.

Here's a seven point summary:

- The accents are of two placements: above the letters and below.
- Those below define a scale. Those above are ornaments.
- There are two closely related sets of accents, one for the 21 books and one for the three books.
- They define music for whole sections of Scripture.
- The music connects verses and chapters both adjacent and separated.
- The music can be understood through the tonality it expresses and the musical phrases it defines. Such understanding suggests ways of hearing the text that would otherwise be missed.
- The music is the third major assist in interpreting the text. It complements the other two: parallelism and word recurrence. There is no conflict among these three.

---

[25] While it would be preferable to have used the Aleppo codex, it was not available to me in a timely and compatible format via web service as is the Leningrad codex.
[26] Many translations would be suitable for underlay. Some would be more difficult than others. My dangerously literal translations and their status may be found at this web address: http://meafar.blogspot.ca/p/psalter-kata-bob.html. All the Music is available in XML form so that brilliant composers and wordsmiths can improve on my halting libretti.

Acknowledgements

No book just happens. There are many influences. There are thousands of people I have depended on for this book, including but not limited to the team who created the Music XML language, and the Music program, Musescore, which reads and formats both XML and Unicode, and the many people who developed Unicode, and the makers of my computer and the Oracle software that runs on it, and the Tanach.us site that made the Leningrad codex available to me, and the staff of Anthony Macauley Associates who created the development environment and helped me with their web service interface that made it so easy to configure and control this specialized project, and the fellows at the University of Victoria in the Centre for Studies in Religion and Society (CSRS) who taught me more about thinking clearly in both scholarship and issues of faith, not to mention the many people with whom I have sung and worshiped and who shaped my life.

On the individual side, I thank particularly Susan Gillingham for introducing the music to me in 2010 at The Oxford Conference on the Psalms and for her continuing encouragement, and David Mitchell for the performances at the conference and for his own clear work cited in these pages, and my first Hebrew teacher Gidi Nahshon of blessed memory, my friend and Hebrew coach, Jonathan Orr-Stav who is always ready to answer a question on the Hebrew language or script, and Jon Wheeler, Haïk-Vantoura's editor, who assisted me greatly with my early learning from her theory, and Ken Behrens, who researched the accents in the 1990's before techniques for automated transcription were available. Of my colleagues at CSRS, Tim Personn, Graduate Student Fellow, read an early draft and helped me formulate my objectives; Harold Coward, former director of the Centre, read a near-complete draft and was very encouraging in his comments. Francis Landy, retired professor of Hebrew studies at the University of Alberta, helped me start my work on Isaiah merely by his love of the tradition.

References

Adler, Cyrus, and Cohen, Francis L. http://jewishencyclopedia.com/articles/3986-cantillation.

Anonymous. 1744. The Majesty and Singular copiousness of the Hebrew Language Asserted and Illustrated. In Eighteenth Century Collections Online, via the University of Victoria Library.

Behrens, Kenneth. 1990s. The Vowel Mantra of the Gospel to the Egyptians and the interpretation of the Masoretic te'amim and other ancient cryptic symbols as musical notation, unpublished manuscript.

DeHoop, Raymond, 2013. The System of Masoretic Accentuation and Colometry in the Hebrew Bible. Oudewater, The Netherlands. https://www.academia.edu/1468512/The_System_of_the_Masoretic_Accentuation_in_the_Hebrew_Bible.

DeCaen, Vincent. 2005. On the distribution of Major and Minor Pause in Tiberian Hebrew in the Light of the Variants of the Second Person Independent Pronouns. Journal of Semitic Studies L/2.

Dotan, A. 1967. The Diqduqé Hatt'amim of Aharon ben Moshe ben Asher. Jerusalem, Masorah, EJ 16, 1401-82.

Dresher, Bezalel Elan. 1994. The Prosodic Basis of the Tiberian Hebrew System of Accents, Linguistic Society of America, Language, Vol. 70, No. 1.

General synod of the Anglican Church of Canada. 1963. The Canadian Psalter.

Gesenius, Kautzsch, Cowley. 1909. Hebrew Grammar.

Haïk-Vantoura, Suzanne. 1976. The Music of the Bible Revealed: The Deciphering of a Millenary Notation (in French).

– 1991. The Music of the Bible Revealed: The Deciphering of a Millenary Notation. John Wheeler (Editor), Denis Weber (Translator).

Heller, Charles. 2006. What to Listen for in Jewish Music. Ecanthus Press.

Jacobson, Joshua R. 2002. Chanting the Hebrew Bible, The Complete Guide to the Art of Cantillation, The Jewish Publication Society.

Kugel, James L. 1981. The Idea of Biblical Poetry, Parallelism and its history. Yale University Press.

Levin, Saul. 1994. The מתג according to the practice of the early vocalizers. State University of New York at Binghampton.

– 1998. The Masoretic Chant of the Hebrew Bible. AJS Review 23 (1). [Cambridge University Press, Association for Jewish Studies]: 112–16. http://www.jstor.org/stable/1486738.

Levy, Elizabeth and Robinson, David. 2002. The Masoretes and the Punctuation of Biblical Hebrew, British and Foreign Bible Society. http://lc.bfbs.org.uk/e107_files/downloads/masoretes.pdf

MacDonald, Bob. 2013. Seeing the Psalter, Patterns of Recurrence in the Poetry of the Psalms, Energion Publications.

– 2014. "Using Software to Analyse Patterns of Recurrence in the Poetry of the Psalms", Journal of Religion, Media and Digital Culture 3(3), pp.129-148. [online] Available at: http://jrmdc.com/papers-archive/volume-3-issue-3-december- 2014/.

Margolis, Max L. 1911. The Place of the Word-Accent in Hebrew, Journal of Biblical Literature, Vol. 30, No. 1. http://www.jstor.org/stable/3259030.

Martín-Contreras, Elvira and Miralles-Maciá, Lorena. 2014. The text of the Hebrew Bible: From the Rabbis to the Masoretes, Vandenhoeck & Ruprecht.

Mitchell, David. 2012. http://home.scarlet.be/~tsf07148/theo/Resinging.pdf, published in the Journal for the Study of the Old Testament 36/3.

– 2013. How can we sing the Lord's Song? Deciphering the Masoretic Cantillation in Jewish and Christian Approaches to the Psalms: Conflict and Convergence, ed. Susan Gillingham, OUP.

– 2015. The Songs of Ascents: Psalms 120 to 134 in the Worship of Jerusalem's Temples, Campbell Publications.

Mulder, Martin Jan and Sysling, Harry (ed.). 2004. Mikra, Text, Translation, Reading and Interpretation of the Hebrew Bible in Ancient Judaism and Early Christianity. Hendrickson.

Reuchlin, Johann. 1518. De accentibus, et orthographia, lingua Hebraicae, à Iohanne Reuchlin Phorcensi … libri tres cardinali Adriano dicati, https://archive.org/details/bub_gb_vCxCn36grhYC.

Revell, E.J. 1971. The Oldest Evidence for the Hebrew Accent System. Bulletin of the John Rylands University Library of Manchester, Volume 54. http://www.jstor.org/stable/416739.

– 1976. Biblical Punctuation and Chant in the Second Temple Period. Journal for the Study of Judaism, Vol. VII, No. 2.

– 2012. The occurrence of Pausal Forms. Journal of Semitic Studies LVIII.2.

Richter, Helmut. http://www.mechon-mamre.org/c/hr/intro.htm#purp.

Rubin, Emmanuel. http://scholarworks.umass.edu/cgi/viewcontent.cgi?article=1000&context=music_faculty_pubs.

The Hebrew Student 2 (5/6). 1883. Antiquity and Authority of the Hebrew Accents. University of Chicago Press: 164–69. http://www.jstor.org/stable/3156048.

Tomalin, Marcus. 2009. Contextualising Accents And Alphabets In The Work Of Christopher Smart, The Review of English Studies, 11/2009, Volume 60, Issue 247. http://www.jstor.org/stable/405771.

Weil, Daniel Meir. 1995. The Masoretic Chant of the Hebrew Bible. Jerusalem: Rubin Mass.

Werner, Eric. 1982. Review of: La musique de la bible révélée; une notation millénaire décryptée, premier recueil: 14 mélodies essentielles, accompagnement pour cordes pincées. Notes 38 (4). Music Library Association: 923–24. doi:10.2307/939998. http://www.jstor.org/stable/939998

Wickes, William. 1881, 1887. 1970. Two treatises on the accentuation of the Old Testament. Ed. Orlinsky, with a prolegomenon by Aron Dotan.

Yarchin, William. 2015. Were the Psalms Collections at Qumran true Psalters? In Journal of Biblical Literature, 134, no. 4.

Appendix 1 Selected Lectionary Components

Deuteronomy 8.6-18, Year A Thanksgiving

11 הִשָּׁמֶר לְךָ נָתַן אֲשֶׁר הַטֹּבָה הָאָרֶץ עַל אֱלֹהֶיךָ
nai e-lo-hei-ka al ha-a-rets ha-to-vah a-sher na-tan lak hi-
weh / your God over the good / / / land that he gives to you. Keep
שְׁמֹר לְבִלְתִּי אֱלֹהֶיךָ יְהוָה אֶת תִּשְׁכַּח פֶּן לְךָ
sha-mer le-ka pen tish-kach et ado-nai e-lo-hei-ka le-vil-ti she-
watch for your-self lest you fog-get / Yah-weh / your God. / so as not to
מְצַוְּךָ אָנֹכִי אֲשֶׁר וְחֻקֹּתָיו וּמִשְׁפָּטָיו מִצְוֹתָיו
mor mits-vo-taiv u-mish-pa-tav ve-chu-qo-tav a-sher a-no-ki me-tsau-
keep his com-mand-ments and his judgments and his stat-utes which I / am / com-
תִּבְנֶה טוֹבִים וּבָתִּים וְשָׂבָעְתָּ תֹּאכַל 12 פֶּן הַיּוֹם
ka ha-yom pen to-kol ve-sa-va-ta u-va-tim to-vim tiv-
manding you to-day. Lest you eat and are satisfied, and you build / good /
וְכֶסֶף יִרְבְּיֻן וְצֹאנְךָ 13 וּבְקָרְךָ וְיָשָׁבְתָּ
neh ve-ya-shav-ta uv-qar-ka ve-tso-ne-ka yir-be-yun ve-
houses and are set-tled. And your herds and your / / flocks / in-crease and
14 וְרָם יִרְבֶּה לְךָ אֲשֶׁר וְכֹל לָךְ יִרְבֶּה וְזָהָב
ke-sef ve-za-hav yir-beh lak ve-kol a-sher le-ka yir-beh ve-
sil-ver and / gold increase for you, and all that is / yours in-creases. And ex-
הַמּוֹצִיאֲךָ אֱלֹהֶיךָ יְהוָה אֶת וְשָׁכַחְתָּ לְבָבֶךָ
ram le-va-ve-ka ve-sha-kach-ta et ado-nai e-lo-hei-ka ha-mo-tsi-a-
alt-ed is your heart, and you for-get / Yah-weh your / God who brought you /
עֲבָדִים מִבֵּית מִצְרַיִם מֵאֶרֶץ
ka mei-e-rets mits-rai-yim mi-beit a-va-
forth from the land of / Egypt, from the house / of
נָחָשׁ וְהַנּוֹרָא הַגָּדֹל בַּמִּדְבָּר 15 הַמּוֹלִיכְךָ
dim ha-mo-li-ka-ka ba-mid-bar ha-ga-dol ve-ha-no-ra na-
servitude. Who / led / you in the great and fear-ful wil-der-/ ness of in-

1 Samuel 17.31-49, Year B Season after Pentecost

38 וַיַּלְבֵּשׁ שָׁאוּל אֶת דָּוִד מַדָּיו וְנָתַן

mak va-yal-beish sha - ul et da-vid ma-dav ve - na - tan
with you. / And Saul / cloth-ed David with his armour and gave him a

39 וַיַּחְגֹּר שִׁרְיוֹן אֹתוֹ וַיַּלְבֵּשׁ רֹאשׁוֹ עַל נְחֹשֶׁת קוֹבַע

qo-va ne - cho-shet al ro - sho va-yal - beish o - to shir - yon vayach-
helmet of brass / for his head. And he clothed him with a breastplate. / And

כִּי לָלֶכֶת וַיֹּאֶל לְמַדָּיו מֵעַל חַרְבּוֹ אֶת דָּוִד

gor da-vid et char - bo mei-al le-ma-dav va-yo-el la - le-ket ki
Da-vid wore his sword ov-er his / ar-mour and he attempted to walk, for he

בָּאֵלֶּה לָלֶכֶת אוּכַל לֹא שָׁאוּל אֶל דָּוִד וַיֹּאמֶר לֹא נִסָּה

lo ni-sah va-yo - mer da-vid el sha-ul lo u-kol la - le-ket ba-
had not tried it out. And Dav - id / said to / Saul / I can-not walk in /

כִּי לֹא נִסִּיתִי דָּוִד וַיְסִרֵם מֵעָלָיו

ei - leh ki lo ni - si - ti vai-si - reim da - vid mei - a -
these that I have not / tried / out. And / David put them aside from

40 וַיִּקַּח מַקְלוֹ בְּיָדוֹ וַיִּבְחַר לוֹ חֲמִשָּׁה חַלֻּקֵי

lav va-yi-qach maq-lo be-ya-do va-yiv-char lo cha-mi-shah cha-lu -
him. And he took his stick in his hand / and he chose / his five /

אֲבָנִים מִן הַנַּחַל וַיָּשֶׂם אֹתָם בִּכְלִי הָרֹעִים

qei a - va - nim min ha-na-chal va-ya-sem o - tam bik-li ha-ro -
smooth / / stones from the wa - di and he set them in the in-ner pouch of the

אֲשֶׁר וּבַיַּלְקוּט לוֹ וְקַלְעוֹ בְּיָדוֹ וַיִּגַּשׁ

im a - sher lo u-va-yal - qut ve - qal - o ve-ya - do va-yi -
shep-herds that was his and in / picking-up with his sling in his hand, he made

Psalm 96, Christmas, all years, Year C, proper 4

Psalm 118, Easter, all years

Appendix 2 Comparing cantillation schemes

Jacobson

All examples are to be sung at a comfortable relative pitch. Haïk-Vantoura assumes a scale from low c (d for the 3 books) to C with tonic on E for all books. Several modes are possible with her scheme. Jacobson has notation that assumes a tonic F for Torah and D for Haftarah. This would imply a d minor natural scale for the latter and an F scale (without B flat) for Torah. The score for Haïk-Vantoura is on the left below, and for Jacobson, on the right.

Zephaniah 3.8 has the property that it uses all the letters. It does not use all the cantillation symbols but it has a substantial selection.

לָכֵן חַכּוּ־לִי֙ נְאֻם־יְהֹוָה
לְי֖וֹם קוּמִ֣י לְעַ֑ד
כִּ֣י מִשְׁפָּטִי֩ לֶאֱסֹ֨ף גּוֹיִ֜ם לְקׇבְצִ֣י
מַמְלָכ֗וֹת לִשְׁפֹּ֤ךְ עֲלֵיהֶם֙ זַעְמִ֔י כֹּ֖ל
חֲר֣וֹן אַפִּ֑י
כִּ֗י בְּאֵ֣שׁ קִנְאָתִ֔י תֵּאָכֵ֖ל כׇּל־
הָאָֽרֶץ׃

Therefore you tarry for me, this is an oracle of Yahweh,
to the day of my arising to the booty.
For my judgment is to gather nations, to collect kingdoms, to pour out on them my indignation, all my fierce anger,
for in the fire of my jealousy, all the earth will be devoured.

For Jacobson, each set of accents *operates as a group*, so the cantor must look ahead to decide what notes to sing. Jacobson uses a libretto of accent names. It is a clever method of teaching this Ptolemaic universe.

: The Sof Pasuk is real punctuation as text. It is not a note. Sof Pasuk marks the division between verses. Two signs are the major disjunctives, the atnah and the silluq.

le - ad

לְעַד Atnah, coming to a rest. It is **Under** the syllable and comes to the fourth note above the tonic. With Haïk-Vantoura it is the subdominant, the fourth note above the tonic.

Atnah is a cadence. While more explicit in Haïk-Vantoura, it appears that traditional cantillation (Jacobson) reflects the same ending and requires a pause, in Haftarah ending on the fourth note of the scale, in Torah on the second note. Jacobson does not deal with the 3 books.

ha - a - rets

הָאָרֶץ Silluq, separation. It is **Under** and returns to the tonic. The silluq always occurs at the end of a verse. It is the same sign as the meteg, and it is hard to tell which is which. The silluq can also occur in the middle of a verse. This is troublesome for those who think of the accents as punctuation.

The sequence for Zephaniah 3.8, step by step, to the cadence is: mahpakh, pashta, zaqef-qatan, tipeha, munah, atnah.

la - kein

לָכֵן Mahpakh, inverted. It is **Under** changing the reciting note to a 6th above the tonic, whether minor or major depends on the mode. In Haftarah (right) it is a descending fourth, In Torah a descending fifth, in each case returning to the tonic D or F.

la - kein

Torah seems influenced by the modern dominant. While the fifth note is used in Haïk-Vantoura, a five-one cadence is not a common feature of the modality. The sequence B E occurs in about 15% of the verses of the whole Bible.

 **חֲכוּ־לִי** Pashta, extending, post. It is **Over** the syllable. The post ornament is the same note+1 (0 1). The traditional melisma on לִי might be something like the pashta shown, i.e. a rise of the fifth.

 **נְאֻם־יְהוָה** Zaqef qatan, small upright. It is **Over** the syllable. The ornament begins on the note below the reciting note and returns to the reciting note: -1 0.

 לְיוֹם Tipeha, handbreadth. It is **Under** the syllable, the third # above the tonic, sharpened in mode 1. In Jacobson, it is a return via a minor triad to the tonic.

Jacobson does not interpret the signs below or above the notes as being significantly different. The tipeha seems like a Haïk-Vantoura qadma.

 קוּמִי Munah, sustained horizontal. It is **Under** the syllable, the fifth above the tonic. Munah appear for Jacobson to be simply stress or sometimes a change in note.

 לְעַד Atnah, coming to a rest. It is **Under** the syllable, the fourth above the tonic. Here there may be some possibly accidental agreement between the systems.

Following the rest is the sequence of accents to return to the silluq:

 כִּי Merkha, prolonged. It is **Under** the syllable, the fifth above the tonic.

Here Jacobson gives three possible interpretations of merkha, from g to e, or the

top half of the first inversion of the major triad, or an extended melisma starting and ending on the same note. The Torah melisma is quite florid.

 מִשְׁפָּטִי Telisha Qetana, small drawing out. It is **Over** the syllable, the ornament, 1 2 3. The right-leaning telisha is quite different for Jacobson from this left leaning one. This may be a misprint for pazer.

le - e - sof

le - e - sof

לאסֹף Qadma, proceeding. It is **Over** the syllable, the ornament, 1 0. For Jacobson, Qadma represents another change of note. For Haïk-Vantoura it is simply an ornament that returns to the reciting note.

go - yim

go - yim

גוֹיִ֜ם Geresh, expulsion. It is **Over** the syllable, the ornament 0 2. Traditionally, this appears to be an ornament that begins and ends on the current reciting note. However, as noted, there is no concept of a variable reciting note in traditional cantillation.

le - qav - tsi

le - qav - tsi

לקַבְצֵ֥י Munah. Haïk-Vantoura does not find a repeated accent significant. It is common enough for a munah to be repeated when one is already on that reciting note. As such it just acts as an accent and not a new note.

mam - la - kot

mam-la - kot

ממלכות Revia, resting. It is **Over** the syllable, the ornament 0 -1.

lish - pok

lish-pot

לשׁפֹּ֤ך Qadma, proceeding. It is **Over** the syllable, the pre-ornament, 1 0. Equally there is little similarity between Torah and Haftarah cantillation.

a - lei - hem

a - lei - hem

עליהֶם Mahpakh, inverted. It is **Under** the syllable, the 6th above the tonic.

za - mi

za - mi   l

זעֲמִי֙ Pashta, extending. It is **Over** the syllable, the post-ornament 0 1.

kol

kol

כֹל֙ Yetiv, resting. It is **Under** the syllable, the 6th above the tonic. Haïk-Vantoura makes no distinction between yetiv and mahpakh. In the one example on page 637, Jacobson shows a yetiv with effectively no change of pitch, perhaps just an extension of the time on a note.

חרון Munah. It is **Under** the syllable, back to the 5th note above the tonic.

cha - ron

cha-ron

אפ֓י Zaqef qatan, small upright. It is **Over** the syllable, the ornament -1 0.

a - pi

a - pi

כ֚י Yetiv, resting. It is **Under** the syllable, return again to the 6th.

ki

ki

בא֣ש Munah.

be - eish

be - eish

קנא֔תי Zaqef qatan.

qin - a - ti

qin - a - ti

תאכ֖ל Tipeha, handbreadth. It is **Under** the syllable, the return to the raised third

tei - a - keil

tei - a - keil

כל־הארץ Silluq is **Under** the syllable, the return home to the tonic.

kol ha - a - rets

kol ha - a - retz

I have found other traditions online. They teach by rote and without rationale for the melismas. But that is to be expected. The Jewish encyclopedia article cited in Chapter 1 above has a series of images that outline many traditions and their florid divergences. Regrettably, none of these is memorable for a first time or even a multiple-time hearer. The melismas do not allow the hearer to memorize the melody or the sense. The Haïk-Vantoura scheme, in contrast, has many memorable phrases. These are memorable because of the changes in reciting note and the hearer's natural perception of both fundamental and secondary harmonics. The patterns are aurally distinguishable and the resulting music aids us as hearers in hearing the ancient word, which is for many, the word of God, and so eminently desirable to be known.

The two interpretations from Jacobson and Haïk-Vantoura can be examined below.

Figure 16 Traditional Cantillation Zephaniah 3.8

Figure 17 Zephaniah 3.8 Haïk-Vantoura

McKorkle

musicofthebible.com has a deciphering key. I have not looked at it closely. It does not succeed in the test for *tonus peregrinus* that Mitchell (2015 :153) suggests concerning Psalm 114. It also does not distinguish between the signs under and over the text.

Behrens

Ken Behrens starts with the key that Haïk-Vantoura started with and changes little. I am grateful to him for bringing to my attention other aspects of ancient musical theory such as the dominance of a four-note scale concept. His scale is Tone, Semitone, tone then tone, and tone, semitone, tone, but with a flattened sixth for the trumpet. This is one of several possible modes, essentially the diatonic minor under Modes above.

He uses, in his own words: 'a vowel "mantra" contained in a Christian pseudepigraphal work called the "Gospel to the Egyptians". By demonstrating this as a likely cryptographical key, and by comparing to other world music cultures, he deduces a scale similar to, but slightly different from Haïk-Vantoura, which is cryptanalytical only. Using the new scale for cheironomy insights, he analyzes the upper te'amim as hand positions as signaling the size of the interval by which to modify the note. His work is not published, but may be obtained from him through his Facebook page.'[27]

In some cases, this reversal of munah and merkha may be slightly easier to sing. It makes less difference in the poetry books because the recitation on the fifth is more common in the prose books, and the poetry default mode is easier to sing than the prose modes anyway.

The change of the two notes weakens the drama in many prose passages where the progression of reciting notes is from the fifth note to the sixth. Recitation on the fifth juxtaposed with recitation on the sixth is frequent in the prose books and the switch of the two notes weakens the impact of the music considerably. While we may be accused of imposing a modern ear onto an ancient mind, I think that the fundamental interval relations of octave (2:1) and perfect fifth (3:2) would have been well-known to the ancients, and I doubt that the ancient ear would have been unable to perceive natural harmonics.

A second weakness that applies to poetry is the lack of an effective cadence on ole veyored. His scheme would leave the singer poised on the dominant rather than the supertonic.

His scheme does not pass the *tonus peregrinus* test. Here is Psalm 114 with his suggested change to the deciphering key. I have used Haïk-Vantoura's ornaments. It is less like *tonus peregrinus* than that of Haïk-Vantoura. In particular, it lacks the beginning on the fifth, it loses the descending sequence of reciting notes, and it overemphasizes a dominant tonic relationship that would be imposing a modern harmonic concept onto the music.

Figure 18 Psalm 114.1-2 with an alternative key

Reuchlin

Medieval work on the accents is evident in this volume in the online archives by Johann Reuchlin (1518 :165). You can read the accent names in the Hebrew, MYRKA, TPHH, ATNH, SVP PSVQ, TLYSHA QTNH, and so on, very roughly transliterated. It looks on the surface as if these are intended for four part homophony. In principle, these could all be programmed into an automated score. All accents appear to be melismatic.

---

[27] From an email conversation, with permission.

Figure 19 Reuchlin, Discantus

Figure 20 Reuchlin, Bassus

Weil

Daniel Meir Weil has put forward a new theory on the original music in his book *The Masoretic Chant of the Hebrew Bible*. The opening paragraph of a book review by Saul Levin is a striking introduction to the problem of new alternative theories: "Never before have I found a book so hard to review. The learned author spent years researching the most complex material, and probably even more time working out an original theory to account for all the ramifications. The result is a methodical, challenging, but frustrating illustration of the perils of scholarship: how a conscientious researcher, while doing his best to explain everything, can still baffle his readers and lose them."

From what I have seen of Weil's thesis, he uses the idea of a chain, 'a concrete psycho-musical entity of reference in the performance' (Weil :4.83). In other words, a 'chain' is a sequence of accents together with a direction to a goal, but one that may be delayed through what he calls a 'back-slip'. Why *chain* and *slip*? Doesn't the idea sound like a musical phrase with a touch of agogic ornamentation, in one case approaching the sub-dominant, and in the other approaching the tonic?

As an example, the pattern that we saw Exodus 3.14 in Chapter 2, recitation on the high C followed by e-g-B-e-A, occurs in 10 verses: Genesis 28.5, Exodus 3.14, 32.12, Jeremiah 11.15, Ezekiel 12.20, 33.31, Hosea 10.15, 1.7, Zechariah 6.1, Ezra 8.33.

Here are three examples that Weil uses.

Genesis 1.9 e B rev,pas,ger,C qad,qad,B z-q,g# ^A e e. This sequence of accents occurs once only. The pattern to the atnah occurs a second time in Genesis 37.14. If we drop the ornaments, the pattern e B C B g A occurs 147 times in the prose books.

Genesis 7.21 e tar,B B rev,C qad,B z-q,g# B ^A g# e. Again as a verse, this is unique. So is the approach to the atnah. Drop the ornaments and the pattern occurs 155 times.

Deuteronomy 12.21 e pas,ger,rev,pas,ger,B zar,B B seg,tar,B e rev,pas,C qad,z-q,g# ^A e qad,z-q,g# f e. This also is unique as is the approach to the atnah. This pattern occurs 15 times.

For common patterns in both poetry and prose see Appendix 3.

Separation of the function of the supra-linear and sub-linear signs is critical to understanding the sequences in each. This underlines the importance of paying attention to the consistent placement of these signs by the Masoretes. If we fail to separate them, we cannot see patterns because there are 16,689 distinct sequences of accents. That is not a useful decomposition of the target problem space.

With Haïk-Vantoura's key, the musical language allows us to show frequency of length of recitation by syllable count and reciting note.

Books	Count	c	d	e	f	g	A	B	C
The 3	4	4	27	372	457	1040	552	501	71
	5		12	181	306	534	448	405	75
	6		6	85	292	182	290	236	42
	7		5	66	288	37	143	74	73
	8		2	43	189	11	45	23	61
The 21	4	753	1296	2659	3378	5808	1336	3744	1282
	5	161	398	1845	682	1670	886	3917	1736
	6	24	70	1257	137	267	575	3327	1560
	7	1	9	923	58	18	395	1969	1357
	8	2	7	769	64		368	1122	1313

Figure 21 Frequency of recitations by syllable count and note

Minor deviations

Mitchell (2015) has argued for some differences with the key that Haïk-Vantoura has for some ornaments. These are the ole-veyored (ole followed by merkha f#) and the revia-mugrash. I have also changed the first, but less radically than Mitchell.

The ole-veyored can occur on several reciting notes theoretically from d through C except A (by definition). But there are no occurrences on g and only 1 on B. My interpretation differs from Haïk-Vantoura in using the lower octave for C but in this I am arbitrary and it does not seem necessary, for it is of rare occurrence in any case.

Figure 22 Ole-veyored, as programmed

Figure 23 Ole-veyored (Mitchell)

Mitchell (2015 :269) has redesigned the pair of ornaments as a run of a descending fifth to the f# no matter what the reciting note we are coming from. Note that we are always approaching the f#, this being the reciting note for the merkha. And note that the combination of merkha following ole only occurs in the 3 books.

Some of the instances of rare cases (from C) are not in the edition that Haïk-Vantoura used for her work. The Leningrad codex agrees with the Aleppo codex.

I find Psalm 45.8 as programmed to be interesting word-painting.

Reciting note	Psalms	Proverbs	Job
d	148	4	12
e	109	12	10
f	69	11	13
B	(45.8) 1	0	0
C	16	0	(7.11, 37.6) 2

Figure 24 Occurrences of ole-veyored by reciting note

Haïk-Vantoura does not observe the paseq, a vertical bar | which may occur anywhere. According to Lea Himmelfarb (Martín-Contreras and Miralles-Maciá :200), the paseq indicates a pause. It is found only in the Tiberian tradition but in the Babylonian tradition, additional disjunctives may be observed in its place. If you note such requests for pause, even where it seems unnecessary, there can be no harm to the drama of the music. May the choir director decide.

PSALM 45

The ole-veyored occurs in a verse by itself or prior to the atnah.

The revia-mugresh also occurs only in the 3 books. Mitchell (2015 :267) thinks that Haïk-Vantoura is close but he has considered the ornament as resembling a baroque trill.

The revia and the zaqef-qatan are not significantly different from each other. Both are similar to a mordent. Differences in interpretation are bound to arise in performance practice.

Appendix 3 Statistics

Tonality

To get a sense of the tonality per the key as inferred by Haïk-Vantoura, the sequences of reciting notes are listed by their musical name. When it comes to ornamentation, to get a sense of the density of the melismatic quality of the music implied in the following tables, I have used the Hebrew accent names, or a three-character abbreviation.

Sequence of notes approaching ^	Count (Prose)	Count (Poetry)
e B A		601
g B A		504
e B g B A	774	467
e f A		464
e g B A	699	444
e B g A	639	315
e f g A (four-note scale)	1079	
e f g B A	769	
e g A	718	
e B f g A	560	
as part of an approach		
… e f g A	1563	0
… e B g A	811	323

If one is designing a key, then how one selects which accent goes with which note may be helped by how frequently each accent occurs in a particular sequence. Suppose one considered that a four-note scale was foundational to the music of the period, then one might look for that scale in the sequences. Or suppose one considered that fifth and fourth would have been common in tuning stringed instruments, or to match natural resonances in a wind instrument like a shofar, then one might look for these intervals.

Here are the sequences of notes used to approach the mid-verse atnah and having more than 500 total occurrences (omitting verses that have no mid-verse cadence, 254 in the 3 books and 1384 in the 21 books).

Frequency of Intervals to ^	Count (Prose)	Count (Poetry)
e A (4th)	1150	219
f B	200	23
B f	2858	3
g C	2	3
C g	1022	41
e B (5th)	6861	1617
B e	2376	120
f C	18	15
C f	910	120
e C (6th)	4212	322
C e	1517	333
d B	5	4
B d	499	45
e g B (triad)	1395	532
B g e	227	72
f g B (dim triad prose)	3123	12
C-c descending octave	71	n/a
B-c descending 7th	501	n/a

There are 23,151 verses in the Hebrew Bible in the Leningrad codex. Of these 1638 have no atnah, roughly 7%. The 3 books have 4502 verses (932 without ornaments), the 21 have 18,649 (2256 without ornaments). Overall the four-note scale occurs more often in the Haïk-Vantoura key than it would if re and sol were reversed. This together with the rendition of tonus peregrinus seems to clinch the decision in favour of Haïk-Vantoura, if indeed the four-note scale is significant. Changing the second with the fifth, f with B, also changes the frequency of the intervals used in the music.

Sequence of notes returning to the tonic	Count (Prose)	Count (Poetry)
f g e	1571	
g e	1304	
g f e	1207	
f g f e	1008	
B g f e	756	
B g e	731	
B f g e	553	
d f g e	424	
C b g f e	384	
C b f g e	309	
f e		1414
g B e		887
e		614
B e		387
e f e		339
f B e		224

These statistics are provisional but I doubt that they will change materially. I have worked closely with about 40% of the text to date (2016). I estimate another 3 years before I finish a first complete translation of the whole of the text. For process and status, please refer to the web pages.

Searching for other patterns, I note that one verse in the poetry has no silluq: Psalm 37.32. Similarly, in the prose books, Numbers 25.19 has no second half of the verse. So there are anomalies in the data that may get verified and corrected as I come to the verse. There are verses that do not begin on the tonic. Why should there not be two that do not end on the tonic? Each of these instances is covered by a note at tanach.us.

The main cadence in the prose books is the atnah with its rest on the subdominant. The ole-veyored is a secondary cadence in the poetry books. This type of cadence occurs 343 times in Psalms, 27 in Proverbs, and 37 in Job. The cadence is not superior or stronger than the cadence on the subdominant, but it can occur in verses without that cadence, 45 times in Psalms, 2 times in Proverbs, and 4 times in Job. Articles and books asserting that the ole-veyored disjunction is stronger than or somehow superior to the atnah are not supported by the data.

The longest recitatives on a single note are Nehemiah 10.40 with a recitation of 51 syllables, 2 Kings 23.4, 55 syllables, and Judges 10.6, 62 syllables.

NEHEMIAH 10

Reciting note	Verses
d	0
e	174
f	936
A	1717
B	0
C	2

Figure 25 The revia-mugresh

Nehemiah 13.5 has an example of a poetry sublinear accent in a prose book. This poetic accent, galgal (differently coded #1450), occurs 16 times: Numbers 35.5, Joshua 19.51, 2 Samuel 4.2, 2 Kings 10.5, Jeremiah 13.13, Jeremiah 38.25, Ezekiel 48.21, Esther 7.9, Ezra 6.9, Nehemiah 1.6, Nehemiah 5.13, Nehemiah 13.5, Nehemiah 13.15, 1 Chronicles 28.1, 2 Chronicles 24.5, 2 Chronicles 35.7. My program may be wrong to ignore these.

Figure 26 Poetic accent in Nehemiah 13.5, ignored

The Top 40 in the Psalms

There are very many possible statistical tables that can be produced. Here are most used sequences of sub-linear accents in the Psalms. The top 40 account for 1,395 of 2,527 verses. There are a total of 706 different patterns of sub-linear accents in the verses of the Psalms. Of these 481 occur only once.

The problem with these statistics is that they are verse by verse, the very same problem outlined in chapter 1. The real challenge now is for us to hear how the verses are put together in a musical form and how the music supports the words in their form. To do this, we need to perform the music and learn how to hear the musical shape, the constructed form for the Psalms, or the chapters of any other book, in their context.

Music	Frequency of Verses	Accent Sequence	Example Psalm
e B ^A f e	102	silluq munah ^atnah merkha silluq	10.17
g B ^A f e	97	tifha munah ^atnah merkha silluq	102.12
e f ^A f e	92	silluq merkha ^atnah merkha silluq	10.18
e B g B ^A f e	73	silluq munah tifha munah ^atnah merkha silluq	10.1

e g B ^A f e	63	silluq tifha munah ^atnah merkha silluq	10.9
g B ^A g B e	61	tifha munah ^atnah tifha munah silluq	104.11
e B ^A e	58	silluq munah ^atnah silluq	102.17
e f ^A e	57	silluq merkha ^atnah silluq	103.3
g B ^A e	57	tifha munah ^atnah silluq	102.18
e B g ^A f e	55	silluq munah tifha ^atnah merkha silluq	10.4
e B ^A g B e	52	silluq munah ^atnah tifha munah silluq	103.5
e B g ^A e	42	silluq munah tifha ^atnah silluq	103.2
e f ^A g B e	42	silluq merkha ^atnah tifha munah silluq	103.9
e g B ^A g B e	39	silluq tifha munah ^atnah tifha munah silluq	102.25
e B ^A B e	34	silluq munah ^atnah munah silluq	104.4
e B g B ^A g B e	33	silluq munah tifha munah ^atnah tifha munah silluq	1.6
e f e	31	silluq merkha silluq	106.6
B g B ^A f e	28	munah tifha munah ^atnah merkha silluq	103.10
e B ^A e f e	28	silluq munah ^atnah silluq merkha silluq	109.3
e f ^A e f e	28	silluq merkha ^atnah silluq merkha silluq	106.41
e g B ^A e	27	silluq tifha munah ^atnah silluq	104.20
g B ^A B e	27	tifha munah ^atnah munah silluq	102.21
e B g ^A g B e	25	silluq munah tifha ^atnah tifha munah silluq	104.32
e B g B ^A e	20	silluq munah tifha munah ^atnah silluq	102.22
g B ^A e f e	20	tifha munah ^atnah silluq merkha silluq	10.15
e B g B ^A B e	18	silluq munah tifha munah ^atnah munah silluq	101.4
e B g B ^A e f e	18	silluq munah tifha munah ^atnah silluq merkha silluq	102.16
B g B ^A g B e	15	munah tifha munah ^atnah tifha munah silluq	108.11
e f ^A f B e	15	silluq merkha ^atnah merkha munah silluq	10.10
e B g B ^A f B e	14	silluq munah tifha munah ^atnah merkha munah silluq	115.6
e B g f e	14	silluq munah tifha merkha silluq	119.103
e f ^A B e	14	silluq merkha ^atnah munah silluq	106.42
B ^A f e	13	munah ^atnah merkha silluq	108.2
e B g ^A B e	13	silluq munah tifha ^atnah munah silluq	104.30
e B g ^A e f e	13	silluq munah tifha ^atnah silluq merkha silluq	102.15
e C B ^A f e	13	silluq mahpakh munah ^atnah merkha silluq	109.25
B ^A g B e	11	munah ^atnah tifha munah silluq	103.8
e f e ^A f e	11	silluq merkha silluq ^atnah merkha silluq	102.8
e g B ^A e f e	11	silluq tifha munah ^atnah silluq merkha silluq	102.5
g f e	11	tifha merkha silluq	119.12

Ornamentation

Excluding merkha-kefula (10 occurrences).

Book	qad	pash	ger	rev	paz	zar	tar	z-q	z-g	seg	tel	qar	shl
Genesis	1015	409	232	544	28	72	109	1201	167	72	141	0	3
Exodus	803	344	216	448	29	81	94	922	94	81	130	0	0
Leviticus	560	278	165	277	27	55	74	648	55	55	126	0	1
Numbers	764	362	205	419	33	94	109	905	105	94	132	1	0
Deuteronomy	668	350	220	429	34	68	107	757	68	68	179	0	0
Joshua	456	274	199	296	48	36	64	507	45	36	174	1	0
Judges	492	224	168	282	27	43	57	542	62	43	115	0	0
1 Samuel	653	321	224	383	32	40	72	722	68	40	148	0	0
2 Samuel	515	218	162	322	29	24	59	568	71	23	133	1	0
1 Kings	620	336	206	397	41	42	77	687	80	42	184	0	0
2 Kings	555	306	205	384	37	47	77	604	70	47	182	1	0
Isaiah	943	242	133	349	22	26	76	1040	61	25	90	0	1
Jeremiah	1036	474	325	620	65	63	174	1144	99	63	263	2	0
Ezekiel	966	392	259	546	56	70	104	1064	128	70	182	1	0
Hosea	134	26	16	54	0	2	10	158	20	2	6	0	0
Joel	57	9	7	30	0	1	6	61	6	1	3	0	0
Amos	98	40	26	45	3	4	17	105	5	4	14	0	1
Obadiah	16	4	3	6	0	0	1	18	1	0	3	0	0
Jonah	36	8	8	19	1	1	4	42	2	1	5	0	0
Micah	81	15	9	38	0	1	10	90	5	1	8	0	0
Nahum	33	9	4	11	0	0	0	43	3	0	2	0	0
Habakkuk	38	2	2	14	0	1	1	42	5	1	1	0	0
Zephaniah	42	11	11	23	1	0	3	46	1	0	5	0	0
Haggai	25	17	11	12	5	0	3	30	3	0	9	0	0
Zechariah	160	61	40	108	7	11	22	180	26	11	31	0	0
Malachi	51	24	17	27	3	1	1	51	9	1	9	0	0
Job (1,2,42)	36	21	15	24	3	6	4	40	1	6	12	0	0
Song	100	12	8	25	0	1	4	108	6	1	1	0	0
Ruth	71	29	17	38	1	2	5	75	8	2	19	0	0
Lamentations	124	31	8	23	0	1	3	133	1	1	4	0	0
Qohelet	141	48	26	57	6	2	14	178	17	2	25	0	0
Esther	134	79	56	93	16	13	27	150	15	13	61	1	0
Daniel	287	120	88	187	27	21	40	322	38	21	75	0	0
Ezra	166	79	52	112	18	16	30	211	31	16	60	1	1
Nehemiah	258	131	97	149	31	21	37	305	32	21	82	4	0
1 Chronicles	572	192	109	257	43	23	58	687	52	23	114	1	0
2 Chronicles	652	337	225	408	55	68	103	693	89	66	199	2	0

Figure 27 Frequency by verse of ornaments in the text of the prose books

Book	qadma/ pashta	revia-mugresh	geresh	revia	illuy	pazer	ole	zarqa	shalshelet
Psalms	280	139	1661	1932	136	72	343	363	29
Proverbs	28	43	637	668	13	10	27	30	4
Job (3-41)	44	58	654	731	20	8	36	42	6

Figure 28 Frequency by verse of ornaments in the text of the poetry books

Note Job 3-41 also excludes the first verse where the narrator speaks, since that narration uses the prose accents. This is not the case after chapter 30.

The Song in the Night

Psalm 16 is a rare example of this ornament pair, revia-mugrash, on the C reciting note.

Common patterns of supra-linear signs, the ornaments, are also important to look at. We already know there are 19,963 verses with at least one ornament. Of these, there are 7506 verses with at least two ornaments in a row without an intermediate change in reciting note. Of these, there are 2717 verses where there are at least 3 ornaments in a row, 874 where there are at least 4 in a row, 315 with at least 5, 104 with at least 6, 28 with at least 7, 14 with 8. This is the maximum number in a row that I have found without an intervening sublinear accent, even though that accent may be the same as the current reciting note (1 Chronicles 5.24 or Jeremiah 51.12). In each of the following tables the accent group is the first column, the frequency the second, and an example in the third. You can see the great complexity required to give 'rules' for sequences of accents even when these are separated from the sublinear accents. That's because such explanations are trying to explain music. Music is not explicable in those terms.

Accent repeated pair	Verses	Sample verse
qadma qadma	3656	Zephaniah 3.6
pazer pazer	43	Numbers 9.5
zaqef-gadol zaqef-gadol	38	Zechariah 6.6
zaqef-qatan zaqef-qatan	27	Song 8.6
revia revia	20	Psalms 97.5
zarqa zarqa	11	Judges 18.14
illuy illuy	5	Psalms 85.1

Figure 29 Ornament pairs that repeat on their own

Qadma occurs 99 times as a trio without other accents intervening, and 11 times as a quad. Pazer 14 times as a trio and once as a quad.

The following tables are sorted on the first accent, then the frequency descending, then the remaining accents.

Accent quad	Verses	Sample verse
illuy pashta revia zarqa	1	Psalms 142.4
pashta geresh revia qadma	254	Zephaniah 3.17
pashta geresh revia telisha	49	Zechariah 5.9
pashta geresh revia tarsin	16	Numbers 21.23
pashta geresh revia zarqa	13	Numbers 35.25

132

Accent quad	Verses	Sample verse
pashta geresh revia pazer	6	Nehemiah 9.8
pashta illuy revia zarqa	1	Psalms 137.7
pashta pazer illuy revia	1	Psalms 40.13
pazer telisha pashta geresh	260	Zephaniah 2.9
pazer pashta geresh revia	2	Jeremiah 39.16
pazer illuy pashta zarqa	1	Psalms 32.6
qadma zaqef-gadol telisha pashta	20	Nehemiah 8.14
qadma zaqef-gadol pashta geresh	14	Zechariah 12.6
qadma zaqef-gadol revia pashta	7	Qohelet 1.16
revia telisha pashta geresh	65	Leviticus 24.3
revia qadma zaqef-gadol zaqef-qatan	11	Ruth 2.9
revia pazer telisha pashta	9	Nehemiah 9.8
revia qadma zaqef-gadol pashta	7	Judges 20.17
revia qadma pashta geresh	5	Jeremiah 51.62
revia qadma telisha pashta	4	Ezekiel 12.25
revia pashta geresh qadma	2	Exodus 9.14
revia qadma zaqef-gadol tarsin	1	2 Chronicles 16.6
segol telisha pashta geresh	34	Qohelet 8.17
segol pashta geresh revia	24	Numbers 21.23
telisha pashta geresh revia	421	Zephaniah 1.10
zaqef-gadol telisha pashta geresh	15	Numbers 15.25
zaqef-gadol pashta geresh revia	7	Ruth 2.11
zaqef-gadol telisha tarsin pashta	2	Zechariah 8.9
zarqa segol pashta geresh	23	Leviticus 2.2
zarqa segol revia qadma	21	Numbers 26.57
zarqa segol telisha pashta	20	Zechariah 14.4
zarqa segol revia pashta	7	Jeremiah 36.14
zarqa segol zaqef-qatan qadma	2	Judges 9.37

Figure 30 Ornaments occurring four in a row

Accent trio	Verses	Sample verse
geresh revia qadma	277	Zephaniah 3.17
geresh revia pashta	96	Zechariah 3.2
geresh qadma zaqef-gadol	4	Numbers 14.29
illuy pashta revia	13	Psalms 97.8
illuy pashta zarqa	12	Psalms 84.3
illuy revia zarqa	2	Psalms 43.4
illuy shalshelet zarqa	1	Psalms 65.2
pashta geresh revia	1016	Zephaniah 3.17
pashta geresh telisha	28	Numbers 3.39
pashta illuy revia	21	Psalms 96.13
pashta revia zarqa	5	Psalms 78.8
pashta revia ole	4	Psalms 9.21
pashta pazer revia	3	Psalms 7.6
pashta zaqef-gadol zaqef-qatan	3	Zechariah 11.9
pashta zarqa revia	3	Psalms 42.5
pashta revia revia	2	Psalms 133.2

Accent trio	Verses	Sample verse
pashta pazer geresh	1	Exodus 20.10
pashta pazer zarqa	1	Psalms 132.11
pazer telisha pashta	353	Zephaniah 2.9
pazer illuy revia	9	Psalms 79.2
pazer pashta geresh	8	Joshua 22.9
pazer telisha tarsin	3	Ezekiel 37.25
pazer geresh pashta	2	Joshua 18.28
qadma zaqef-gadol zaqef-qatan	202	Zechariah 5.6
qadma zaqef-gadol pashta	143	Zechariah 12.6
qadma zaqef-gadol revia	75	Ruth 2.19
qadma zaqef-gadol telisha	33	Zechariah 8.9
qadma zaqef-gadol tarsin	28	Song 7.13
qadma telisha pashta	14	Leviticus 8.15
qadma zaqef-gadol zaqef-gadol	13	Nehemiah 13.13
qarne telisha pashta	6	Numbers 35.5
revia qadma qadma	574	Zephaniah 3.6
revia qadma zaqef-gadol	260	Zephaniah 3.19
revia telisha pashta	176	Zechariah 5.9
revia pashta geresh	169	Zechariah 1.6
revia qadma pashta	19	Leviticus 22.3
revia pazer telisha	13	Nehemiah 9.8
revia telisha tarsin	8	Leviticus 10.4
revia zarqa segol	7	Numbers 23.3
revia pazer pazer	5	Nehemiah 7.7
revia qadma tarsin	4	2 Chronicles 32.30
revia tarsin pashta	4	Joshua 7.2
revia geresh pashta	3	Judges 2.17
segol pashta geresh	65	Zechariah 8.14
segol telisha pashta	52	Zechariah 14.4
segol qadma qadma	23	Judges 16.26
shalshelet pashta geresh	1	Genesis 19.16
shalshelet qadma qadma	1	Genesis 39.8
shalshelet revia qadma	1	Genesis 24.12
telisha pashta geresh	1542	Zephaniah 3.8
telisha tarsin pashta	10	Zechariah 8.9
telisha geresh pashta	1	2 Samuel 14.15
telisha revia pashta	1	Jeremiah 36.11
tarsin revia qadma	7	Numbers 18.9
tarsin revia pashta	6	Numbers 36.13
zaqef-qatan qadma qadma	5	Numbers 3.33
zaqef-qatan telisha pashta	5	Exodus 34.32
zaqef-qatan pashta zaqef-gadol	2	Genesis 12.7
zaqef-gadol qadma qadma	176	Zephaniah 2.2
zaqef-gadol revia qadma	66	Zechariah 14.8
zaqef-gadol telisha pashta	65	Qohelet 8.17
zaqef-gadol pashta geresh	46	Zechariah 12.6
zaqef-gadol revia pashta	21	Qohelet 7.14

Accent trio	Verses	Sample verse
zaqef-gadol zaqef-qatan zaqef-qatan	13	Numbers 7.5
zarqa segol revia	57	Zechariah 14.5
zarqa segol pashta	31	Numbers 27.7
zarqa segol qadma	26	Numbers 5.13
zarqa segol telisha	22	Zechariah 14.4
zarqa segol tarsin	14	Nehemiah 10.30
zarqa segol zaqef-qatan	8	Judges 9.37
zarqa segol pazer	3	Judges 9.15
zarqa revia ole	1	Proverbs 23.35

Figure 31 Ornaments occurring three in a row on their own

Accent pair	Verse	Sample Verse
geresh revia	1102	Zephaniah 3.17
geresh pashta	127	Zephaniah 3.5
illuy revia	60	Psalms 97.7
illuy pashta	32	Psalms 97.8
pashta geresh	3229	Zephaniah 3.8
pashta zaqef-gadol	320	Zechariah 6.6
pashta revia	84	Psalms 97.8
pashta zarqa	75	Psalms 96.10
pashta pazer	14	Psalms 7.6
pazer telisha	407	Zephaniah 2.9
pazer zarqa	17	Psalms 99.9
pazer tarsin	15	Qohelet 8.11
pazer illuy	11	Psalms 79.2
pazer revia	7	Psalms 71.3
pazer geresh	6	Joshua 18.28
qadma zaqef-gadol	6513	Zephaniah 3.8
qadma pashta	69	Zechariah 7.12
qadma revia	24	Zechariah 4.12
qadma tarsin	21	Leviticus 9.7
qarne tarsin	2	Ezra 6.9
revia qadma	2242	Zephaniah 3.6
revia pashta	740	Zephaniah 3.8
revia telisha	268	Zechariah 7.12
revia tarsin	158	Zechariah 4.10
revia zarqa	141	Psalms 89.53
revia ole	134	Psalms 97.10
revia geresh	42	Zechariah 8.12
revia pazer	24	Nehemiah 9.8
segol revia	128	Zechariah 9.15
segol pashta	101	Zechariah 8.14
segol qadma	92	Ruth 4.4
segol telisha	58	Zechariah 14.4
segol tarsin	39	Numbers 8.19
segol geresh	15	Numbers 1.50
segol zaqef-qatan	13	Judges 9.37

Accent pair	Verse	Sample Verse
segol pazer	10	Numbers 11.18
shalshelet illuy	4	Psalms 3.3
shalshelet zarqa	4	Psalms 72.3
shalshelet qadma	2	Genesis 39.8
telisha pashta	2308	Zephaniah 3.8
telisha tarsin	92	Zechariah 8.9
telisha geresh	22	Nehemiah 9.15
telisha qadma	3	Judges 11.36
telisha revia	2	Jeremiah 36.11
tarsin pashta	67	Zechariah 8.9
tarsin revia	42	Numbers 7.81
tarsin telisha	6	Nehemiah 5.18
zaqef-qatan qadma	24	Numbers 3.33
zaqef-qatan pashta	13	Leviticus 15.18
zaqef-qatan revia	8	Joshua 22.28
zaqef-gadol qadma	967	Zephaniah 3.19
zaqef-gadol zaqef-qatan	697	Zechariah 7.3
zaqef-gadol pashta	368	Zechariah 6.1
zaqef-gadol revia	252	Zechariah 6.10
zaqef-gadol telisha	109	Zechariah 8.9
zaqef-gadol tarsin	65	Zechariah 2.4
zaqef-gadol geresh	16	Jeremiah 32.29
zarqa segol	351	Zechariah 14.5
zarqa ole	1	Psalms 45.8

Figure 32 Ornaments occurring in pairs on their own

Note, these verse counts are accurate for the combinations listed, but I may have missed a rare combination in that I took my model pairs, trios and quads only from their first occurrence in a verse. The point is made, however, that music is simply too complex to analyse in terms of accent sequences, even when you distinguish between the accents under and over the text. Music is like language. It goes beyond what we can say about it.

Reconciling names

Reconciliation with Wickes is nigh impossible. Ben Asher has a series of differing names also. Wickes distinguishes the same sign in its slightly altered position as different. You can see that sometimes the very same sign can be disjunctive or conjunctive. This does not seem reasonable for a human reader. More so, he speaks of one accent morphing into another (1887 :20). This is simply not possible unless a manuscript starts behaving like something out of Hogwarts. If he refers to differing manuscripts having different signs, then that is editorial and must reflect whatever visual, grammatical or musical bias we have in a particular copyist for whatever textual reason.

Sometimes Haïk-Vantoura (or my program does based on my reading of her work) makes a distinction for ornaments based on the position, as can be seen in the Music column. The Music column for ornaments is the shape of the ornament, quarter if one note, eighths if 2, a triplet if 3, or two triplets if 6. +n means above the reciting note, -n below, +/- zero is equivalent.

Name	Unicode	Music	Sign	Interpretation	Class (Wickes)	in
darga	1447	c	בְ	scale, (trill – there are several trills per Wickes)	conjunctive	21
tevir	1435	d	בֶ	broken note	disjunctive	21
silluq	1469	e	בֽ	end, returning	d	24
merkha	1445	f (#)	ב֥	lengthening, prolonging	c	24
tifha	1430	g(#)	ב֖	handbreadth	d	24
tifha	1453	g(#)	בֹ		c (mayla)	3
atnah	1425	A	ב֑	from נוח causing to rest	d	24
munah	1443	B	בֻ	also called shofar, surely the fifth is appropriate, being a natural overtone	d or c (!)	24
mahpakh	1434	C	ב֢	inverted shofar turned round	c	24
yetiv	1444	C	ב֚	resting	d (!)	24
galgal	1442	d#	בֶ	wheel, moon a day old	c	3
galgal	1450	ignored	בֶ		c	21
qadma	1433	+0+1	בֹ	going on	c (azla)	21
pashta	1448	+1-0	בֹ	extending	d (!)	24
geresh	1436	+0+2	בֵ	expulsion	d	21
geresh	1437	+2-0	בֵ		d	3
tarsin	1438	+2+0+2	בֵ	double geresh	d	21
pazer	1441	+2+1	בֵ	tremble, shake or trill, conspicuous (Ben Asher)	d	24
zaqef-qatan	1428	-1	בֺ	upright small	d	21
zaqef-gadol	1429	-1-2	בֺ	upright large	d	21
revia	1431		בֺבֺ	revia-mugrash, always in the second part of a verse	d	3
revia	1431	-1+0	בֺ	resting	d	3
revia	1431	-0-1	בֺ	not distinguishable except by book	d	21
segol	1426	-1-0-1	ב֒	named after the vowel	d	21
zarqa	1454	-0-1+1	ב֮	not listed in treatise 2	c (tsinnor)	24
zarqa	1432	-1+1-0	ב֮	to sprinkle, scatter	d (!)	24

137

Name	Unicode	Music	Sign	Interpretation	Class (Wickes)	in
telisha	1449	+1+2+3	בֿ	Wickes considers disjunctive for this as bad taste!	c (little)	21
qarne	1439	+1+2+3 +3+2+1	בֿ	not mentioned - rare	d (great pazer)	21
telisha	1440	+3+2+1	בֿ	pluck out, draw out	d (!)	21
illuy	1452	+4	בֿ	suspended, shake	c	3
ole	1451	+3+0	בֿ		d	3
ole-veyored	1451, 1445	+3+0	בֿבֿ	ascending and descending	d	3
shalshelet	1427	-3-2-1	בֿ	ascending chain	d	24

Index of Musical Examples and Cited Authors

CPSIA information can be obtained
at www.ICGtesting.com
Printed in the USA
LVOW01s2352151116
513127LV00001B/1/P